CONSPIRACIES
OF WORLD WAR II
DEVIOUS PLOTS, SINISTER SABOTEURS AND EXTRAORDINARY ENIGMAS

T0016853

ALEXANDER MACDONALD

This edition published in 2023 by Arcturus Publishing Limited
26/27 Bickels Yard, 151–153 Bermondsey Street,
London SE1 3HA

AD010539UK

Printed in UK

CONTENTS

INTRODUCTION

World War II was itself a conspiracy. That, at least, was one of the charges that the top Nazis faced at the Nuremberg Trials. Conspiracy to wage wars of aggression was also one of the charges levelled at Japan's leaders at the Tokyo War Crimes Trial of 1946–48.

The prosecution at Nuremberg charged the defendants on four counts – crimes against peace, crimes against humanity, war crimes or violations of the laws of war, and 'a common plan or conspiracy' to commit the criminal acts outlined in the first three counts. The conspiracy extended to the propagandists who created the ideological basis for the war, the genocide of the Jews and other crimes, and to the industrialists without whom it would not have been possible for Germany to wage war.

However, the judges ultimately limited the last of these charges to 'conspiracy to wage an aggressive war'. On this basis, only those who had attended key meetings planning the war in 1937 and 1939 were convicted. This was a refutation of the prosecution's contention that the conspiracy began with the founding of the Nazi Party in 1920. The judges instead ruled that it began with the creation of the so-called Hossbach Memorandum, a summary of a meeting in Berlin on 5 November 1937 named after army adjutant Colonel Friedrich Hossbach, who took the minutes. The memorandum records that, at the meeting, Adolf Hitler said he did not want war with Britain or France, but that he did favour a number of small wars of plunder to boost the struggling German economy.

From the Nazi point of view, of course, the war was started by an international conspiracy of wealthy Jews seeking to dismember Germany. This can be discounted. The overwhelming majority of Jews murdered in the death camps were hardly wealthy. More than half the Jews who died in the Holocaust were from the Soviet Union.

Hitler, meanwhile, had come to power in Germany using conspiracy, infiltrating Nazi sympathizers into the police and legal system. This gave his militia of Storm Troopers, the *Sturmabteilung* or *SA*, commonly known as the Brownshirts, the freedom to openly commit acts of violence, intimidation and even murder on the streets of Germany with little fear of prosecution, while those that opposed them were jailed.

He consolidated his power by conspiracy, too. Four weeks after Hitler was appointed Chancellor in January 1933, the Reichstag (Germany's parliament building) was burnt down. Hitler claimed that this was part of a Communist conspiracy and immediately began to arrest known and suspected Communists and closed down their offices, meeting places and newspapers. The day after the fire, at Hitler's request, President Hindenburg signed the Reichstag Fire Decree that suspended most civil liberties in Germany, including habeas corpus, freedom of expression, freedom of the press, the right of free association and public assembly, and the secrecy of the post, telegraph and telephone.

Hitler's bodyguard, the *Schutzstaffel* (or *SS*), was given police powers 'for the protection of the people and the state'. Twenty-five thousand *SS* officers took to the streets alongside the regular police force and rounded up political opponents. Soon, the jails were filled to overflowing and prisoners were herded into hastily constructed concentration camps.

This was all done in the run-up to an election scheduled to take place less than one week after the Reichstag fire. In the ballot on 5 March 1933, the Nazi Party increased its share of the vote from 33 per cent to 44 per cent and, with the help of the small German National People's Party, was able to secure a parliamentary majority. The Nazis promptly passed an Enabling Act giving Hitler's cabinet the authority to enact laws without parliament's approval for four years. The Act also removed presidential oversight. Over the next three months, all political parties other than the Nazis were banned.

However, the Communists claimed that the Reichstag fire had been part of a conspiracy by the Nazis to discredit them. Five Communists had been arrested after the fire and charged with arson. Although four of them were acquitted at trial, one of them, Dutchman Marinus van der Lubbe, was convicted and executed. His actual role in the incident remains unclear. Van der Lubbe did admit to starting the fire, but his confession could have been obtained under the influence of drugs or torture. In 1955, former *SA* member Hans-Martin Lennings revealed that his unit of Storm Troopers had collected van der Lubbe from a hospital on the night of the fire and brought him to the Reichstag. When they arrived, he testified in a sworn affidavit, the fire already appeared to be lit and there was 'a strange smell of burning and there were clouds of smoke billowing through the rooms'. Although he did not admit it, and perhaps did not know, it was probably the case that Lennings and his *SA* colleagues had been sent to pick up van der Lubbe, a trade unionist and known Communist, to provide a suitable scapegoat for a conflagration that had in reality been started by the Nazis themselves.

Interestingly, at the Nuremberg trials, General Franz Halder testified that Hermann Göring himself admitted responsibility for starting the fire. Halder said that, at a luncheon held on Hitler's birthday in 1942, Göring admitted that 'the only one who really knows about the Reichstag is I, because I set it on fire!' In his own Nuremberg testimony, Göring denied the story – though, as president of the Reichstag at the time of the fire, he did have access to a tunnel that ran from his official residence to the parliament building. What all of the claims and counter-claims achieve is uncertainty, which is the hallmark of any good conspiracy. Historians to this day continue to debate van der Lubbe's involvement or otherwise in the fire and whether he was framed, tricked into starting the blaze, or guilty as charged.

To maintain power, Hitler even conspired against his own supporters. In the summer of 1934 he and his inner circle had the leadership of the *SA* murdered, fearing that Ernst Röhm, the head of what was effectively a private army of street fighters, was a threat to his authority now that he was in office. This action became known as the 'Night of the Long Knives' and was also carried out to appease senior officers in Germany's armed forces,

The Reichstag fire – a Communist conspiracy or the work of the SS?

the *Wehrmacht*, who saw the *SA* as a rival. Hitler knew that, having won power with the help of the *SA*, he no longer needed its support as much as he needed that of the armed forces now that he was planning to wage war. At least 85 were killed during the initial round of the purge, which began on 30 June and would go on to consume hundreds of victims.

During his rise to power, Hitler had promised the German people *lebensraum*, or living space, by taking territory in the east. To do that, he needed an excuse to attack Poland. This was provided by a false-flag operation organized by the *SS* and known as the Gleiwitz Incident. On the night of 31 August 1939, a small group of German *SS* men dressed in Polish uniforms led by *SS Sturmbannführer* Alfred Naujocks took over a radio station in Gleiwitz, which was then in eastern Germany (and is now in Poland and is known as Gliwice), and began to broadcast anti-German propaganda in Polish. This ended with the sound of gunfire, as if the station was being stormed.

To make the attack look more convincing, Naujocks' unit had with them the dead body of Franciszek Honiok, a German Silesian and known Polish sympathizer, who had been arrested the day before by the Gestapo. Honiok was dressed to look like a saboteur and his dead body riddled with bullets was left at the scene, along with the corpses of inmates from Dachau, their faces disfigured so they could not be identified. They were dressed in Polish uniforms, thought to have been provided by, of all people, Oskar Schindler, then working for the *Abwehr*, or German military intelligence. During the war, Schindler famously saved the lives of some 1,200 Jews and Yad Vashem, Israel's Holocaust memorial, would later honour the industrialist by bestowing upon him the honorific 'Righteous Among the Nations'.

Hitler made a public broadcast to condemn what Nazi newspaper the *Völkischer Beobachter* called an 'unprecedented attack by bandits on Gleiwitz radio station'. Yet before the paper had even published the story the German Army had already crossed the border into Poland. This was the morning of 1 September 1939. When Hitler ignored an ultimatum to withdraw his troops from Poland, Britain and France declared war on Germany two days later.

The war in the Pacific began in a similar fashion, with the Mukden Incident. On 18 September 1931, a Japanese lieutenant set off a small charge of dynamite alongside a Japanese-controlled railway line at Mukden (now Shenyang) in southern Manchuria. Dissidents were blamed and the Japanese Imperial Army invaded and set up the puppet state of Manchukuo, in northeast China. Just 19 countries around the world officially recognized the new nation.

Full-scale war between Japan and China began with the Marco Polo Bridge Incident on 7 July 1937. On this date, the Japanese used the pretext of searching for a missing soldier to cross without permission the Yongding River that marked the border between Manchukuo and China. As Japanese troops went over the Marco Polo Bridge a firefight broke out that soon escalated into full-scale combat. For many, this episode marked the beginning of World War II in Asia – and it's thought that Japan purposely staged it all to give themselves a *casus belli* to take on China.

When Japan launched its attack on the US naval base at Pearl Harbor on 7 December 1941, the whole world reacted with surprise – including the Americans of course, who the following day joined World War II on the side of the Allies. Ever since, there have been rumours and suggestions that certain highly-placed world leaders, among them British Prime Minister Winston Churchill and even the US President Franklin D. Roosevelt, knew the raid was coming but did nothing to prevent it – evidence, it is argued, that both men wanted neutral America to enter the war whatever the cost.

KILLING HITLER

Operation Valkyrie was the best-known conspiracy of World War II. It occurred on 20 July 1944, when Count Claus Schenk von Stauffenberg, a colonel and chief of staff to the Reserve Army Command, attempted to assassinate Hitler by planting a bomb in his headquarters, the Wolf's Lair, in Rastenburg, East Prussia.

But the 20 July plot was not the only attempt on Hitler's life. One of the would-be Operation Valkyrie assassins was Lieutenant Colonel Rudolf-Christoph von Gersdorff who, from April 1941 to September 1943, was an intelligence officer with the Army Group Centre in Russia. It was there that he met Colonel Henning von Tresckow, who was with the general staff and who later recruited Stauffenberg for his bomb plot. Witnessing what he later described as the 'cruel methods used in Russia' that had been advocated by Hitler, Gersdorff wrote in his postwar memoirs that it was 'clear to all that this man deserved death a thousand times'.

By 1942, the circle around Tresckow made up their minds to kill Hitler and if possible to also remove Hermann Göring and SS chief Heinrich Himmler. While other plotters elsewhere were looking at alternative plans – for example, to kidnap Hitler and force a change in Germany's top military leadership – Tresckow was always clear that half-measures like this would simply lead to civil war. Only the shock of the death of the 'mystic Führer' would make it possible for a coup d'état to proceed according to plan.

'It was clear from the beginning that the attempt had to be made in such a manner as to assure absolute certainty of success,' Gersdorff would write. 'And it was axiomatic that the attempt must be carried out as soon as possible.'

An assassination by pistol was ruled out because it was generally believed that Hitler always wore a bullet-proof vest. Tresckow decided that the use of a bomb would give the best chance of success. He asked Gersdorff to prepare the explosive and fuses. His particular requirement was that the bomb should be about the size of a book or a bundle of documents and have sufficient power to destroy a small house and its occupants. It would also need a time fuse that would work with absolute certainty but without any audible ticking.

The device the conspirators ultimately chose came from an unlikely source: an English magnetic mine filled with English explosives that would be detonated by an English fuse. These items had been dropped by enemy aircraft over Germany for use in sabotage by agents and resistance groups and had somehow been acquired by the plotters. 'None of the available German devices were suitable, being either too large or too conspicuous,' Gersdorff wrote. 'Tresckow made many tests with these devices. The power of the explosive seemed quite satisfactory, although naturally it was impossible to make tests with living beings. The fuse was especially suitable because of its rod form and its simple operation – the crushing of a foil cap. There were fuses with a time delay of 10, 30, 120 and 360 minutes. Experiments showed that the surrounding air temperature affected the time delay. At less than room temperature the time delay could be increased by as much as a hundred per cent.' Now that the conspirators had their weapon of choice, they had to wait for a suitable opportunity to use it.

The first assassination attempt was carried out in February 1943 by Tresckow when Hitler visited the Army Group headquarters in Smolensk, in German-occupied Russia. Tresckow was tasked with bringing Hitler from the airfield personally, and he planned to place a bomb in the side pocket of the automobile they would travel in, next to Hitler's seat. Hitler, however, never travelled in cars that were not his own. When Hitler arrived by train in Smolensk his personal vehicle and driver were already waiting for him, and Tresckow was unable to move the bomb he'd prepared from his car to Hitler's.

With the plot to kill Hitler in Smolensk foiled, Tresckow and Gersdorff were presented with another opportunity the following month. On 21 March, Hitler visited an exhibition of captured Soviet arms, equipment and other spoils of war at the Zeughaus, a baroque palace in Berlin being used as an armoury. Gersdorff agreed to attend the *Führer's* visit, during which time he would set off two explosive devices, killing himself, Hitler, and anyone else in close proximity (including, it was hoped, any other high-ranking Nazis who tended to be present at these sorts of official events).

'Before flying to Berlin, I had asked Tresckow to tell me whether the coup d'état could be successfully carried out once Hitler had been assassinated,' Gersdorff wrote in his memoirs. 'Since I did not expect to survive, I wanted to know if my act would be justified in the eyes of history. At that time Tresckow told me that the organization already existed and would go into action immediately, that arrangements had already been made with the Western Powers, and that the enterprise was the only chance to save Germany from complete destruction. Other than this, I knew only that Tresckow was in close contact with various branch chiefs in the Army High Command.'

Gersdorff was flown to Berlin and was informed that, after making an address in the glass-roofed court of the exhibition building, Hitler would spend about half an hour looking at the exhibits, accompanied by Göring, Himmler, Admiral Dönitz and several aides. He would then carry out the traditional review of the honour guard.

After investigating the layout of the Zeughaus, Gersdorff concluded that the actual attempt could only be made during the time Hitler's party was touring the exhibition, a period expected to last at least 20 minutes. With this in mind, on the day of the visit Gersdorff set the fuse timers on his bombs for 15–20 minutes. But, as things got underway, there was a last-minute change of plan. The tour, it was announced, would last no longer than eight minutes. This was too short a period for Gersdorff to reset his explosives – in fact, he barely had time to defuse the bombs once

Hitler and his entourage had left. Without even knowing it, the German leader had unwittingly avoided assassination. 'This last-minute change of schedule, indicative of the extreme precautions that Hitler took, was responsible for saving his life once again,' Gersdorff wrote. It was after this failed assassination attempt that Claus von Stauffenberg joined the conspirators.

Stauffenberg was a veteran of German fronts in Poland, France, Russia and Africa. It was while he was in Tunisia that he was injured, losing his left eye, right hand and two fingers from his left hand. As the war continued, he became convinced Hitler would bring Germany to disaster.

In September 1943, he had been introduced to Tresckow, who was then a staff officer in the Berlin headquarters of the *Ersatzheer* – or 'Replacement Army' – charged with training soldiers to reinforce first line divisions at the front. Another of the Replacement Army's roles, approved by Hitler himself, was to take control of the Reich in the event of internal disturbances that blocked communications to the military High Command. This part of the Replacement Army's responsibilities was known as Operation Valkyrie. Because the *Ersatzheer* was populated by a number of army officers opposed to Hitler's rule, Valkyrie over time was slowly, surely and secretly adapted to become a means by which the German leader's would-be assassins could formulate a plan to assume power once Hitler had been removed.

When it became known that Stauffenberg was sympathetic to the plotters' cause he was attached to the *Ersatzheer* so that he could assume a more central role – especially after Tresckow was posted to the Eastern Front and was no longer able to play an active part in the conspiracy. With Stauffenberg effectively left in charge of the plot, his colleague in the Army Command Major Axel von dem Bussche volunteered to carry out the assassination of Hitler. This was to take place in November 1943, at the Wolf's Lair during a demonstration to the *Führer* of the new winter uniforms. Göring and Himmler were also due to be present, and the plan was for von dem Bussche to kill all of the high-ranking Nazis – and himself – with a suicide bomb made up of a landmine hidden inside his tunic that would be set off by a hand grenade detonator. The details were carefully

Claus von Stauffenberg, the man who very nearly killed Hitler.

worked out, with von dem Bussche even planning to fake a coughing fit at the crucial moment when he moved in to gather Hitler in a final, fatal embrace (to cover the 'fizzing' noise of the detonator's five-second fuse). The assassination never came to fruition, though, as the train bringing the new uniforms to the Wolf's Lair was destroyed in an air raid and Hitler's visit was called off.

Undeterred, von dem Bussche volunteered to carry out another attempt once the new uniforms were ready to be presented in February 1944, but he, like Tresckow, was posted to the Eastern Front before the opportunity arose. When another new uniform presentation ceremony was announced for 7 July 1944, a major general, Helmuth Stieff, was recruited as von dem Bussche's replacement. By this time, the D-Day landings of 6 June had convinced many in Germany's High Command that the war was lost – and that Hitler had to go. But, in the event, 7 July 1944 passed without incident as Stieff backed out at the last moment. Stauffenberg decided that he had no alternative but to remove Hitler himself once a suitable opportunity arose – and it came just under two weeks later.

Despite his very noticeable injuries (or perhaps because of them), Stauffenberg cut an aristocratic and authoritative figure in Germany's military hierarchy. He was one of Hitler's trusted high-ranking officers and his role in the Reserve Army Command meant it was only natural that he be asked to attend a meeting with the *Führer* and other senior officials at the Wolf's Lair on 20 July to discuss troop movements on the Eastern Front. When he arrived on the day, Stauffenberg carried a briefcase containing a powerful bomb primed to explode once proceedings were under way. His plan was to place the briefcase as close as possible to Hitler and slip away on the pretext of making an important phone call. This was not to be a suicide mission; Stauffenberg believed that, as the most senior Army Reserve officer on the ground with detailed knowledge of how Operation Valkyrie should be implemented, he needed to survive in order to ensure Germany would not descend into chaos once Hitler was gone.

As it was a hot summer's day, however, the location of the meeting was changed at short notice from the subterranean (and well-enclosed) concrete *Führerbunker* to a wooden hut. Undeterred, Stauffenberg entered the room and placed the briefcase close to where Hitler would be sitting, resting it against one of the legs of the office's meeting table. He then left the room to make his imaginary phone call and, moments later, the device exploded. Thinking he had succeeded in his mission, Stauffenberg headed back to Berlin.

But the devilishly lucky Hitler had not been killed. He had been shielded from the blast by the heavy oak leg of the meeting room table. He was injured, but suffered only comparatively minor wounds. Rather than cover up the incident, Hitler swiftly turned it into a propaganda coup, claiming that his survival was proof of his destiny to rule the Western world. 'I regard this as a fresh confirmation of the mission given me by Providence to continue toward my goal,' he claimed in a radio broadcast that same night.

Stauffenberg, meanwhile, was already back in Berlin and was beginning to implement Operation Valkyrie with his fellow conspirators. But, with a hesitancy born from years of living under Nazi oppression, and believing that Hitler was dead, they missed their opportunity. Before they could take any meaningful steps towards taking control of the state, the more dynamic Hitler was on the phone to loyal operatives and countermanding their orders. The game was up almost before it began.

Stauffenberg and the other leading plotters were arrested and executed the next day by firing squad. This was not simply ruthless Nazi efficiency at work: the man who ordered their summary execution without a trial or questioning was General Friedrich Fromm, commander-in-chief of the Reserve Army, who was almost certainly aware of the plot and who therefore had a strong vested interest in doing away with its ringleaders before his own compliance in it was revealed. Stauffenberg and the men shot alongside him were the lucky ones. The failed assassination sparked a vicious manhunt that resulted in suspected sympathizers being rounded up, tortured, sent to concentrations camps, beaten, and, in many cases, strangled with piano wire and hung up on meat hooks – a grisly fate that was supposedly filmed so that Hitler could enjoy watching their painful deaths at his leisure.

The 20 July plot unleashed an atmosphere of unprecedented paranoia in the Reich that did little to help its cause in the field. Hitler became more than ever convinced that the army generals were not to be trusted and that his judgement alone should be brought to bear. In the round of reprisals that followed in its wake the state lost some of its most capable military leaders. Chief among these was Field Marshal Erwin Rommel, the Third Reich's most successful general. He had a distant association with Stauffenberg, and this was enough in itself to sign his death warrant (although it's likely that he would have joined with the conspirators had they been successful). Rather than face a trial and execution, Rommel chose to take his own life on 14 October in order to shield his family from any shame or humiliation. Officially, it was reported that he died in a car crash. The battle-hardened experience of the 53-year-old Rommel would be sorely missed in the months to come, especially by his troops in Normandy fighting to stem the Allied advance eastwards after D-Day.

Other high-profile victims of Operation Valkyrie's failure included Stauffenberg's own brother, Berthold, who suffered a slow and agonizing death by strangulation, and General Fromm. His swift executions of Stauffenberg and his colleagues had not been enough to save his skin. Hitler was determined after the attempt on his life to purge the military of all of his enemies, real or perceived. Ultimately, Claus von Stauffenberg, his brother Berthold and Fromm were just three of the 20,000 or so souls who were killed or imprisoned in the aftermath of the assassination attempt.

THE NIGHT OF THE LONG KNIVES

Those who conspired against Adolf Hitler should have been well aware of the price they would pay for failure. Throughout his career the *Führer* had shown that he was utterly ruthless and would conspire against even his closest allies if that was what suited him.

Ernst Röhm was an early member of the Nazi Party. He had been an ally of Hitler since the early 1920s and was a co-founder of the brown-shirted *Sturmabteilung*, or *SA*, the 'muscle' the Nazis used to protect party rallies and to disrupt the meetings of their rivals. Under Röhm, the Brownshirts played a key role in bringing Hitler to power. So key, in fact, that the *Führer* came to see Röhm as a rival. In 1934, Hitler had Röhm murdered during a military and political purge known as the 'Night of the Long Knives'. The *SA* lost much of its power and was replaced by the unimpeachably loyal *Schutzstaffel*, or *SS*, each of whose members personally swore allegiance to Hitler himself.

Röhm was a career soldier. He was born in 1887 and, at 18, he joined Royal Bavarian 10th Infantry Regiment Prinz Ludwig at Ingolstadt as a cadet. Within two years, he had reached the rank of lieutenant and by the outbreak of World War I he was an adjutant. He was injured three times during the conflict, earning an Iron Cross First Class after sustaining a serious chest wound at the Battle of Verdun in 1916. More a soldier than an officer, he condemned the cowardice, sensuality and other vices of many of his comrades; as a working-class boy, he was viewed with suspicion and some scorn by the supposedly better-bred officer class that he became a part of.

By the end of the war he was a captain. He remained in the military and was assigned to the army's special intelligence section in Munich, a unit tasked with keeping a watchful eye over the many political groups that sprang up in Germany after the war. At the same time, he joined the *Freikorps*, the paramilitary force of volunteers that was ostensibly formed to combat the growing influence of Communism in Germany after 1918. Before long, however, the *Freikorps* became a home for disaffected and dispossessed ex-servicemen unhappy with their country's defeat in the war and the 'betrayal' perpetrated on the German people by the victorious Allies and the liberals and intellectuals who now led the state in what was known as the Weimar Republic.

In 1919, in the civil unrest and rebellions in Germany that followed the end of the war, left-wing socialists set up the Bavarian Soviet Republic in Munich. Röhm was among the *Freikorps* troops that in May that year violently suppressed the new revolutionary regime, whose leaders were executed and murdered in short order. The destruction of the Bavarian Soviet Republic was in many respects the open implementation of plans people on the right in Germany had been advocating for months. On 7 March 1919, Röhm met with a 29-year-old World War I veteran named Adolf Hitler who was then still enlisted in the army. Some believe the purpose of the meeting was for Röhm to recruit Hitler as a spy to watch and inform on the left-wing and Communist groups that were springing up around Munich (and which would seize power in the short-lived Bavarian Socialist Republic the following month). Whatever the purpose of their getting together in a dimly-lit beer cellar, Hitler later recalled that theirs was a meeting of minds, and that they spent the evening discussing ways to combat the left-leaning revolutionary movements around them. Both men possessed a burning hatred for the new democratic Weimar Republic and the 'November criminals' of the government they believed were responsible for their country's capitulation that had ended the war. The two of them agreed that in order to build a strong, nationalist Germany the state needed a new party built on people from the lower classes. People like themselves.

Ernst Röhm, who aimed to displace Hitler and paid with his life.

Following the collapse of the Bavarian Socialist Republic, Adolf Hitler was one of the many people arrested as 'red' sympathizers, probably on account of his successful infiltration of left-wing groups as an army informer. It was Röhm who vouched for Hitler, had him released, and then helped the future *Führer* find work teaching courses on history and politics at Munich University. Both Röhm and Hitler also joined the small German Workers' Party, which then had less than 50 members. With his gift for oratory, Hitler was appointed chief of propaganda, while Röhm headed up the group's secret band of murderers – men, it was said, who killed without the slightest qualm. They renamed the Germany Workers' Party the National Socialist German Workers' Party, or Nazi Party, and it became virulently anti-Semitic.

Like many early Nazis, Röhm was gay. One of the accusations levelled against him was that he used his power in order to seduce young recruits. Joseph Goebbels, a reactionary homophobe, later brought Röhm's behaviour to the attention of Hitler, who reacted by declaring: 'Nauseating! The Party should not be an Eldorado for homosexuality. I will fight against that with all my power.'

At the same time, though, Röhm was the only person among his associates who called Hitler 'Adolf' and used the German familiar *du* when addressing him.

By 1921, membership of the Party had swelled to more than 2,000 and Hitler took over the leadership. That September, he was sent to jail for three months for being part of a mob that beat up a rival politician. When Hitler was released, he formed the *SA* as his own private army. Röhm helped his party's leader to organize the new force, recruiting former members of the *Freikorps* for their experience in street-fighting and in using violence against their rivals. As his role grew, Röhm quit the *Reichswehr* to commit himself full-time to the Party.

In November 1923, Hitler led the so-called Beer Hall Putsch, a poorly planned attempt in Munich to take over the government in Bavaria. The uprising was swiftly put down and its leaders arrested. As one of the coup's plotters (he had led a militia that seized the war ministry during the insurrection), Röhm was found guilty of high treason but only received a 15-month suspended sentence. Similarly, as the main ringleader, Hitler was handed a lenient five-year term, but served only nine months. Both the Nazi Party and the *SA* were outlawed, but the ban was easily evaded: the *SA* was rebranded as *Frontbann* and the Nazi Party was renamed the National Socialist Freedom Party (NSFP). In national elections in May 1924, Ernst Röhm was elected to the Reichstag as an NSFP deputy, despite his conviction for high treason. When the law prohibiting the *SA* and the Nazi Party expired in January 1925, the *Frontbann* and the NSFP simply reverted to their old names.

During Hitler's time in prison – a period in which he wrote *Mein Kampf* – Röhm assumed a more prominent role in the Party. This led to tensions between the two men after Hitler was freed at the end of 1924. In 1928, Röhm accepted a job in South America as adviser to the Bolivian Army. Two years later, however, Hitler recalled him to become chief-of-staff of a reorganized *SA*, which now had one million members. This gave Röhm a huge power base within Gemany; but by this time Hitler had also set up the *SS* as his personal bodyguard under the leadership of Heinrich Himmler. It was clear that Röhm was not going to have everything his own way.

Hitler became Germany's chancellor in 1933, and Röhm celebrated the historic event in a speech that carefully referenced both his own organization's and Himmler's roles in the new regime, claiming that, 'A tremendous victory has been won. But not an absolute victory! The *SA* and the *SS* will not tolerate the German revolution going to sleep and being betrayed at the halfway stage by non-combatants. Not for the sake of the *SA* and *SS* but for Germany's sake. For the *SA* is the last armed force of the nation, the last defence against communism.' Within a year Hitler had assumed absolute power in Germany, but if Röhm expected to be rewarded for his loyalty to the *Führer* he was to be disappointed. Rivals such as Himmler assumed prominent places in the new regime, but Röhm remained in charge of what was increasingly seen as an army of street thugs with no clear role in the new German Reich Hitler wanted to establish. The *SA* leader was particularly embittered by Hitler's courtship of the military, whose traditionally aristocratic High Command both men agreed had helped Germany lose the war of 1914–18. 'Adolf is a swine,' Röhm complained. 'He only associates with the reactionaries now. His old friends aren't good enough for him. Getting matey with the East Prussian generals. They're his cronies now ... Are we revolutionaries or aren't we? The generals are a lot of old fogies. They will never have a new idea ... I don't know where he's going to get his revolutionary spirit from. They're the same old clods, and they'll certainly lose the next war.'

Röhm's antagonism to some of Hitler's new friends, and his leadership of a large force of armed men, marked him out as a target. The *Werhmacht* leadership definitely wanted him removed, as did rival Nazis such as Göring and Goebbels. Himmler, who disapproved of the *SA* leader's

SA members in the 1920s who brought Hitler to power, but had to be tamed.

lifestyle, later claimed he had implored him to 'dissociate himself from his evil companions, whose prodigal life, alcoholic excesses, vandalism and homosexual cliques were bringing the whole movement into disrepute'. The fact that the press was at this time openly ridiculing Röhm's sexual preferences helped to weaken his status within the Party, making him vulnerable to attack. When Rudolf Diels, the head of the Gestapo, reported to Hitler that Röhm was plotting against him the *SA* chief's fate was sealed. Hitler had not forgotten the power struggle between himself and Röhm in the mid-1920s that led to the latter's temporary exile to Bolivia. This time around there would be no reprieve for the *Führer*'s old comrade.

Hitler had long suspected Röhm of harbouring left-wing sympathies, and on 4 June 1934 the two men had a five-hour meeting during which the *Führer* told his *SA* leader that some people believed that he was 'preparing a Nationalist-Bolshevik revolution, which could lead only to miseries beyond description'. In response, Hitler decided to eliminate the socialist wing of the Party and tasked Himmler, the newly appointed head of the Gestapo Reinhard Heydrich, Hermann Göring and Theodor Eicke, the commandant of Dachau concentration camp, to draw up a 'Reich List of Unwanted Persons'. The name at the top was Ernst Röhm.

On the evening of 28 June, Hitler called Röhm, ordering him to convene a conference of the *SA* leadership at the Hanselbauer Hotel in Bad Wiessee two days later, assuring him that he would be safe.

The architects of the Night of the Long Knives – Hitler, Göring, Goebbels and Hess.

With all of the *SA*'s senior officers gathered in one out of the way location, Hitler arrived at the hotel at 6.30 am on 30 June, accompanied by a fleet of cars filled with *SS* men. According to Erich Kempka, the *Führer's* chauffeur, 'Hitler entered Röhm's bedroom alone with a whip in his hand. Behind him were two detectives with pistols at the ready. He spat out the words; "Röhm, you are under arrest". Other *SA* officers were rounded up. Those caught in compromising situations were dragged out of their bedrooms and shot in the road. The rest, around 200 men, were taken to Munich's Stadelheim Prison. Röhm's boyfriend, Karl Ernst, the head of the *SA* in Berlin, had just married and was driving to Bremen with his bride to board a ship for their honeymoon in Madeira. Ernst's car was overtaken by *SS* gunmen, who shot up the vehicle, wounding his wife and his chauffeur. Ernst was taken back to *SS* headquarters and executed later that day.

Hitler decided to pardon Röhm because of his past service. However, after pressure from Göring and Himmler, he agreed that Röhm should die. Himmler ordered Theodor Eicke to carry out the task. Eicke and his adjutant, Michael Lippert, travelled to Stadelheim Prison where Röhm was being held. Eicke placed a pistol on a table in Röhm's cell and told him he had 10 minutes in which to use the weapon on himself. Röhm replied: 'If Adolf wants to kill me, let him do the dirty work.'

Ten minutes later, Eicke and Lippert returned to find Röhm standing defiantly in the middle of the cell, stripped to the waist. The two *SS* officers pulled out their revolvers and riddled him with bullets. Eicke later claimed that Röhm fell to the floor moaning: '*Mein Führer.*'

After what became known as the Night of the Long Knives, anyone who dared to oppose Hitler knew exactly what to expect.

CRIME OF PASSION

Hitler was a murderer. Don't hold the front page. We all know that he started a war that killed up to 60 million people, including six million Jews murdered in the Holocaust. However, there was one murder in 1931 that, had it been reported and investigated, would have prevented the whole thing.

The victim was Hitler's 23-year-old niece, Geli Raubal. He got to know Geli in 1927 when he took on her widowed mother, Hitler's half-sister Angela, as a housekeeper at his mountain retreat in Bavaria. Geli was just 19 and idolized the man she called 'Uncle Alf', who was then 38. To get his niece away from her mother's watchful eye, Hitler moved her to his apartment in Munich under the pretext of Geli studying medicine there. She had little interest in medicine, however, and was bored by politics. But the things she was interested in, Hitler would not let Geli do. She was not allowed to go out dancing with people her own age and, once, when Hitler saw her out on the street with a fellow student, he threatened to beat her with the whip he was carrying. He also lectured Geli on the dangers of sexual intercourse in the most graphic detail.

As a young man living in Austria, Hitler had given friends similar lectures after taking them to Spittelberggasse, Vienna's red-light district. Due to the virulent anti-Semitism in Austria at that time, many young Jewish girls unable to find work had been forced into prostitution, sitting half-naked in brothel windows. It is believed that Hitler contracted syphilis in Spittelberggasse, possibly from a Jewish prostitute.

When Geli took a shine to Nazi Party member Otto Strasser, Hitler stopped her from seeing him and resorted to keeping her locked up at night. But this was not enough for Hitler. Convinced that his niece was seeing other men without his knowledge, he accused Geli of being a whore and had her mother Angela take her to a gynaecologist to be examined. When the doctor confirmed that Geli was still a virgin a repentant Hitler bought her an expensive ring – but still kept her under lock and key. Angela, concerned about Hitler's intentions towards her daughter, asked him to promise that he would not seduce her. This should have been the least of her worries. Something far more strange and awful was going on between Hitler and Geli.

One of the many victims of the Night of the Long Knives was Otto Strasser's brother, Gregor. He had angered Hitler by resigning from the Nazi Party in 1932. Concerned for his own safety, Otto Strasser fled to Canada. There, he was interviewed by the psychoanalyst Dr Walter C. Langer, who was preparing a psychological profile of Hitler for America's Office of Strategic Services. Being a Freudian, Langer focused particularly on Hitler's sex life. When his report was finished, it was circulated to Roosevelt and Churchill. What they read surely gave them pause as Strasser's revelations about Hitler's relationship with Geli were nothing short of shocking. 'Hitler made her undress,' he said. 'He would then lie on the floor. She would have to squat over his face where he could examine her at close quarters and this made him very excited … When the excitement reached its peak, he demanded that she urinate on him and that gave him his sexual pleasure. Geli said the whole performance was extremely disgusting to her and it gave her no gratification.'

Strasser also told the psychiatrist that he had been told similar stories by Henriette, the daughter of Hitler's official photographer, Heinrich Hoffman, but had dismissed them as hysterical ravings. Geli, he said, had told a girlfriend that Hitler was 'a monster … you would never believe the things he makes me do'. The chambermaids who had to clean Geli's bedroom, he said, complained about the 'very strange and unspeakable' things that had taken place there.

In 1929, pornographic sketches Hitler had made of Geli fell into the hands of their landlady's son. Father Bernhard Stempfle, a rabid anti-Semite and a friend of Hitler, managed to buy them back. He, too, perished in the Night of the Long Knives.

With Geli safely locked up at night, Hitler was free to go out on the town. One of his favourite haunts was Heinrich Hoffman's photographic studio, a known hangout for homosexuals. Hoffman made pornographic films which Hitler watched there. Hoffman also noted the *Führer's* unhealthy interest in his 16-year-old daughter. During Hitler's absences, Emil Maurice, a founder member of the SS, began seeing Geli. When Hitler discovered that Geli had allowed Maurice to make love to her, he was beside himself with anger. He condemned Maurice as a 'filthy Jew' and forbade Geli from having anything to do with any other man.

Other Nazi Party leaders by now were growing uneasy about Hitler's relationship with his niece. The Party was on the verge of a major electoral breakthrough and a scandal would have wrecked Hitler's chance of seizing power. At the same time, Geli, now 23, was becoming increasingly frustrated after Hitler refused to let her go to Vienna to study music. The situation took on a special urgency when Geli discovered she was pregnant. It is not thought that the child was Hitler's. Pornographic drawings in one of his last letters to Geli indicate that he was impotent (Magda Goebbels later tried to get her own back on her philandering husband, propaganda minister Joseph, by bedding Hitler, but also found he could not rise to the occasion).

Geli's child may have been Emil Maurice's, though she had also slept with the young Nazi assigned to guard her. Worse still, Hitler's nephew, Liverpool-born William Patrick Hitler, claimed that the father was 'a young Jewish art teacher in Linz'.

On the night of 18 September 1931, there was a terrible row as Hitler was preparing to leave for a rally in Nuremberg. Neighbours claimed to have heard Geli shouting to Hitler from their second-floor balcony as he was getting into his car. Hitler shouted back: 'No. For the last time, no.' Geli shut herself away in her bedroom. The next morning, servants broke open the door and found her dead body. She had been shot.

Geli Raubal – was it suicide or was she murdered by Hitler?

The first detective on the scene, Heinrich Müller, quickly ruled out foul play. He later rose to become head of the Gestapo. Wilhelm Gürtner, the Bavarian Minister of Justice, followed this up by hurriedly calling off the investigation. He would go on to become the Reich Minister of Justice. There was no inquest.

The official story was that Geli had committed suicide because she was worried her voice was not good enough to be a singer. Hitler claimed that he was 145 km (90 miles) away in Nuremberg when he heard of Geli's death. He took out a writ against the anti-Nazi *Münchener Post* newspaper which reported that Geli's nose had been broken and other injuries had been sustained in a struggle.

Apart from the *Münchener Post*'s revelations, there were other inconsistencies in the story of Geli's death. Three different people claimed to have broken down the bedroom door. While neighbours claimed to have overheard Geli and Hitler's parting conversation, no one reported hearing a shot. There was no indication that Geli was depressed. She was halfway through writing a letter to a girlfriend when she died – indeed, she was halfway through the word '*und*', German for 'and'. The sentence read: 'When I come to Vienna – hopefully soon – we'll drive together to Semmering an...'

Rigor mortis had sent in and the police doctor estimated that she had actually died the previous evening. The bullet had entered above the heart, passed through her lung and lodged in her lower back at hip level. This meant the gun had to be pointing downwards and the hand holding it had to be higher than her heart, a very awkward way to commit suicide. The pistol used was Hitler's.

Her body was taken down the back stairs of the apartment building, sealed in a lead coffin and smuggled out of the country. Geli was given a Catholic burial in her native Austria, even though to bury a suicide in hallowed ground was against church rules. The priest, Father Johann Pant, wrote to a French newspaper in 1939, saying: 'They pretended she committed suicide. From the fact I gave her a Christian burial you can draw your own conclusions.'

Journalist Fritz Gerlich investigated Geli's murder. He claimed that, instead of leaving for Nuremberg that Friday, Hitler had dined with Geli in a restaurant and that Hitler, who seldom touched alcohol, drank beer. When they went back to the apartment, there was a row and he shot her. According to Otto Strasser, the public prosecutor wanted to charge Hitler with murder, but was overruled. He fled the country when Hitler came to power. Gerlich was murdered for his pains. So was the restaurant owner who said that Geli and Hitler had eaten their last meal together at his place.

Gregor Strasser, who at the time of Geli's death was close to Hitler, said that he had been forced to stop the Nazi Party leader from committing suicide after he shot his niece. This almost certainly contributed to his own murder in 1934 on the Night of the Long Knives – another of whose victims was Strasser's lawyer, Gerd Voss, who held the former Nazi's personal papers containing details of Hitler and Geli's strange relationship.

After Geli was buried back in Austria, Hitler secretly visited her grave one night, spending hours in the cemetery and leaving just before dawn. Later, he commissioned a life-size bust of Geli and wept when it was presented to him. He kept it swathed in flowers and would shut himself away every year on the anniversary of Geli's death.

'Geli's death had such a devastating effect on Hitler it changed his relationship to everyone else,' said his deputy, Hermann Göring.

Nevertheless, the cover-up remained in place throughout Hitler's lifetime. Dr Langer's report on the *Führer's* sexual proclivities was not published until 1972, in *The Mind of Adolf Hitler*. It detailed Hitler's perversions, which were widely known among the top Nazis. If they had been made public at the time it would have fatally damaged his reputation. With the help of his political cronies, Hitler got away with one murder, allowing him to go ahead and commit millions more.

FLIGHT TO SCOTLAND

The facts are straightforward enough. On 10 May 1941, Hitler's deputy Rudolf Hess flew solo for almost 1,600 km (1,000 miles) from Augsburg-Haunstetten airfield in Bavaria in a Messerschmitt Bf110 before parachuting into a field near Eaglesham in Scotland.

Captured by the British, he was held as a prisoner of war, despite claiming he had left Germany on a one-man peace mission to end the war. In 1946, he was put on trial in Nuremberg, convicted and given a life sentence. He was held in Spandau Prison in Berlin – alone for the last 21 years of his life – dying there aged 93 in 1987. But the story of his plane journey has been surrounded by myths and mysteries ever since, provoking numerous conspiracy theories.

When Hess was captured in Scotland, he gave a false name and said he had an important message for Douglas Douglas-Hamilton, the 14th Duke of Hamilton. But Hess had never met Douglas-Hamilton and mistakenly believed that the duke was part of an anti-government faction that opposed the war with Germany – as many British aristocrats had before 1939. When planning his flight, Hess had sought the advice of his old friend Albrecht Haushofer, an academic and diplomat who had met Hamilton at the 1936 Berlin Olympics and had stayed in touch in the years that followed. As he had some Jewish ancestry, Haushofer was alienated from the Nazi regime, but his friendship with Hess had kept him safe – initially. He was arrested after Claus von Stauffenberg's failed 20 July plot in 1944 and executed on the night of 22 April 1945, just after the first Soviet troops entered Berlin.

Rudolf Hess (left) – was his one-man peace mission sanctioned by Hitler?

However, there was no evidence that the Duke of Hamilton had any sympathy with the Nazi cause, or that he was part of an anti-government faction. Indeed, he was a member of the Conservative Party, a friend of Winston Churchill and served in the RAF, then responsible for the air defence of northern England and southern Scotland. In 1942 Douglas-Hamilton won a libel action against two Communists who asserted that he was friends with Hess.

The Soviet leader, Joseph Stalin, for one, had his suspicions on the links between Britain and the Nazis. Hess flew to Britain just a month before Germany launched its surprise attack on the Soviet Union in Operation Barbarossa. Stalin later claimed that Hess made his flight at the behest of British intelligence, which was trying to cook up a peace deal with Hitler before Germany invaded the Soviet Union. The Duke of Hamilton, Stalin thought, was a go-between. Although the attack made Britain and the Soviet Union allies, Stalin's doubts persisted. He could not fathom why Britain did not execute Hess as a war criminal, but put him up in some comfort in a Surrey mansion instead.

On 19 October, *Pravda*, the official newspaper of the Communist Party, reported that, 'It is not coincidence that Hess's wife has asked certain British representatives if she could join her husband. This could mean that she does not see her husband as a prisoner. It is high time we knew whether Hess is either a criminal or a plenipotentiary who represents the Nazi government in England.' A few days later, the paper backed up its allegations by publishing a picture of 'Mrs Hess' in Britain. Embarrassingly for the Soviets, this turned out to be a photograph of Myra Hess, the celebrated English concert pianist who helped raise the country's morale by playing free lunchtime recitals at London's National Gallery.

Nevertheless, Stalin persisted in his belief and even toasted British intelligence for 'inveigling Hess into coming to Britain' at a dinner with Churchill. This theory persisted until the end of the Soviet Union in 1991, when the KGB admitted that, although they believed the Duke of Hamilton was not directly involved in any peace plot, they were aware of fake letters purporting to be from him that were sent to Hess in order to lure him to Britain. These letters had been sent by MI6, the Soviets alleged, and they had been told of their existence by Kim Philby, one of their highly placed double agents operating inside Britain's intelligence services.

In 2004, declassified MI5 files revealed that in early September 1940 Hess had tried to open up a clandestine dialogue with Douglas-Hamilton by asking Haushofer to write to the duke. The files revealed that Hess proposed a meeting in Lisbon in neutral Portugal to discuss a peace agreement between London and Berlin. British intelligence intercepted the letter, however, and considered setting up a sting operation by luring Hess into a trap.

It is not clear if the secret services followed through with their plan, but there are tantalizing glimpses that they may have. Frank Foley was a high-ranking intelligence officer and had been the head of MI6 in Berlin before the war. According to the diary kept by his wife, Kay, on 17 January 1941 Frank Foley and his aide flew out of Whitchurch Aerodrome near Bristol on a clandestine flight to Lisbon. They returned two weeks later, on 1 February.

Kay Foley – and others – believed that her husband met Albrecht Haushofer in Lisbon to reassure him that all was set for the Duke of Hamilton to welcome Hess and that a peace deal was already on the table. All of this was done, apparently, without the duke's knowledge. Why the British secret service would want Hess to come to the UK remains an open question. The likely answer is that Britain wanted to land a major propaganda and intelligence coup by capturing a top Nazi – and one who presumably had access to high-level secret information (although it turned out he did not). The other, less plausible but still possible, response is that there were elements in the secret services that did want to broker some sort of peace deal with a regime in Germany they were not entirely unsympathetic too.

Even at that time, with the war escalating, there were elements of the British elite up to and including members of the royal family that still admired Hitler, and were anxious to forge an accommodation or even an alliance with Germany in order to fight the Soviet Communists who they regarded as more of a threat to their way of life. The links between Hitler and the former Edward VIII and Wallis Simpson are well-documented, but less publicized are the Nazi sympathies of Edward's (and King George VI's) younger brother, Prince George, the Duke of Kent.

A cocaine addict and promiscuous bisexual, the Duke of Kent's lovers included the Soviet spy Anthony Blunt and the singer-actress Jessie Matthews. British intelligence listed him as a person of special interest. On 25 August 1942 the duke took off in a Sunderland flying boat from Invergordon in Scotland, ostensibly bound for Iceland on what was documented as a 'Special Mission – Non-Operational'. Not long into the flight, and while on a route that indicated the final destination was not Iceland, the duke's plane crashed in flames on Eagle's Rock above the small Caithness village of Berriedale. When the duke's dead body was recovered he was found handcuffed to a briefcase filled with 100 Krona Swedish banknotes, which suggests he was actually heading to neutral Sweden, perhaps to meet representatives from Berlin.

By some miracle, the plane's tail-gunner, Flight Sergeant Andrew

Jack, survived the crash. To his dying day, Jack insisted that there were 16 passengers on board the plane and not the 15 listed on the flight manifest. Jack's testimony fuelled suspicions that the additional passenger was Hess. This would mean, of course, that the person sequestered for so long in Spandau was not Hess. As we will see, Jack's assertions were not the last time it was claimed that Hess has somehow avoided imprisonment by death, escape or some other means.

The conventional version of Hess's flight to Britain is that he suffered from some sort of breakdown and undertook his peace mission entirely of his own volition. This implies that Hitler knew nothing of his deputy's plans. This is borne out by Albert Speer, the *Führer*'s personal architect and future Minister of Armaments. He later wrote that Hitler erupted in fury when he heard of Hess's defection, and entries in the diaries of Joseph Goebbels record how Hitler said Hess deserved to be shot as a traitor for his actions.

There are, however, claims that Hitler was well aware of Hess's intentions – and actually approved them. On the night that Hess's flight from the Augsburg-Haunstetten airfield was being prepared, he supposedly handed a note to Karlheinz Pintsch, his senior adjutant, with instructions to pass it on to Hitler. According to Pintsch, Hitler remained calm when he read the note. Although this contradicts Speer and Goebbels's reports of Hitler's rage on discovering his 'betrayal' by Hess, it should be remembered that Pintsch's version of events was given under some duress. After initially being arrested following Hess's defection, Pintsch was sent to the Eastern Front in 1944. Captured by the Red Army, he spent 11 years in an East German prisoner-of-war camp and was repeatedly questioned, sometimes under torture, to reveal what he knew of Hess's mission. The result was a 28-page 'confession' where he claimed his mission was to use all means at his disposal 'to achieve, if not a German military alliance with England against Russia, at least the neutralization of England'. Pintsch's document also stated that Hitler was fully aware of the mission and also claimed that the flight had taken place with the 'prior arrangement of the English'. Given the circumstances under which Pintsch's story was obtained, it is unsurprising that it aligned so perfectly with Stalin's own take of Anglo-Nazi collusion and secret peace deals.

After he landed in Scotland, Hess was actually allowed to meet Douglas-Hamilton, only to be told by the duke himself that he had been misinformed of his sympathies and that any talk of appeasement or peace deals was out of the question. Hess at this point did appear to become slightly unhinged. This is understandable. He did, after all, believe he had flown to what would be a pre-arranged and sympathetic meeting. Now, however, he appeared as nothing more than a deluded lunatic on a fantasy mission.

Having been placed under arrest, Hess was transferred to a series of prisons. One of these was the Tower of London, where he requested – and was denied – a meeting with Churchill. Hess was then sequestered in 'Camp Z', the well-appointed Mytchett Place, a 12-bedroom mansion in Surrey where he was interrogated by MI6. While there a depressed Hess attempted to take his own life by throwing himself down the building's main staircase. He only succeeded in breaking his leg, and, after recuperating, spent the rest of the war being held in the Maindiff Court Military Hospital and POW Reception Centre in Abergavenny, Wales.

One reason many people still question whether Hess acted alone was the nature of his relationship with Hitler. Hess was no fair-weather Nazi. After hearing Hitler speak for the first time in Munich in 1920, Hess was utterly devoted to the *Führer*. The following year, he was injured protecting Hitler from a bomb planted by Communists at a Nazi Party event. After the abortive Beer Hall Putsch of November 1923, Hess was arrested and imprisoned with Hitler in Landsberg Prison, where he edited the *Führer's* autobiographical manifesto, *Mein Kampf*. Hess even named his only son Wolf, which was Hitler's codename. With all this in mind, is it feasible that Hess would have embarked on a one-man peace expedition without Hitler's say so?

It also seems unlikely that Hess could have made the arrangements for his flight without anyone noticing. To reach Britain from Bavaria, the Messerschmitt he used had to be fitted with long-range fuel tanks. To keep the carrying out of these modifications secret from ground staff, mechanics and other pilots would have been difficult.

Of Hess's journey itself, it was remarkably trouble-free. No attempt was made to intercept his unauthorized flight as he passed over occupied Europe. In a highly convenient twist, Hermann Göring, then commander-in-chief of the Luftwaffe, received no news of the flight until Hess was over the North Sea and beyond the Nazis' reach.

There are other puzzling aspects of Hess's flight. The American Consul in Amsterdam reported that Hess had landed at Schiphol Airport to refuel, though there was no mention of his arrival or departure in the airport's log. This was at a time when security at the airport had just been tightened following the theft of a twin-engined Fokker G-1 just five days earlier by two Dutchmen who used it to make their escape to England. What's more, there was no need for Hess to have stopped in Holland at all as he had enough fuel on board to take him across the Channel. In his own account, Hess said he had flown 129 km (80 miles) east of Amsterdam and had not touched down in the Netherlands at all.

More confusingly, on 23 May 1941, the Swedish newspaper *Svenska Dagbladet* published a report stating that Hess had set off from Calais, not Augsburg. This may simply have been a mistake. In another intriguing – if unverified – detail, Hess was allegedly escorted for part of his flight by *SS-Obergruppenführer* Reinhard Heydrich, who at that time was conducting coastal defence missions from the Netherlands.

Then there is the puzzle of how Hess got through British air defences without being attacked or, if peace talks had already been arranged, escorted safely to his destination. There was a heavy air raid on London that night, which would have provided a diversion. But Hess crossed the coast 483 km (300 miles) north of London at 10.23 pm and baled out over Scotland at 11.09 pm. There was no air raid alert at London until 11.02 pm, 39 minutes after Hess crossed the coast.

After his capture, Hess maintained that he had flown to Britain without his *Führer*'s knowledge. An MI5 investigation carried out in Germany in

Rudolf Hess's crashed plane. He survived but remained silent for the rest of his life.

1946 also concluded that Hess had flown on his own initiative and without orders from Hitler. It confirmed that the letter Hess had asked Pintsch to deliver to Hitler stated his intention to obtain a last-minute understanding with Britain before the German offensive on the USSR in June 1941. This was in line with the various peace overtures Hitler had earlier made, where he said that Britain could keep its overseas empire if it allowed Germany a free hand on the Continent. After defeating France in revenge for its victory in World War I, Hitler's main objective in Europe was to secure *lebensraum* ('living space') for German people in the east and the destruction of Bolshevism there.

When the chance came to publicly interrogate Hess on the whole affair at the Nuremberg Trials he proved uncooperative. He complained of amnesia and appeared distracted. He later admitted to feigning madness

– a ruse his doctors saw through and passed him fit to stand trial. After being handed a life sentence, Hess was taken to Spandau Prison, his home for the next 41 years. While incarcerated, he told the Australian journalist Desmond Zwar that he realized Germany could not win a war on two fronts. 'I knew that there was only one way out – and that was certainly not to fight against England,' he said. 'Even though I did not get permission from the *Führer* to fly I knew that what I had to say would have had his approval. Hitler had great respect for the English people.'

During his four decades in prison, there were calls for Hess to be released. One, perhaps outlandish, theory why this never happened was because he held information on top secret Nazi bases in the Antarctic operated by the Vril Society. This was an occult organization (that may or may not have actually existed) whose members believed that a subterranean master race of Aryans – living somewhere beneath the South Pole – had engineered Hitler's rise to power and, after the war, had spirited the still-living *Führer* away to their domain. Here, they were actively plotting Hitler's triumphant return and the inauguration of a Fourth Reich, possibly with the help of UFOs piloted by Vril Society acolytes. As bizarre as this sounds, it's a theory that is given a modicum of credence by the fact that none other than James Bond creator Ian Fleming, who at that time was in naval intelligence, recommended that any interrogations of Hess should be conducted by the infamous necromancer Aleister Crowley.

More prosaically, Hess's prolonged incarceration can be attributed to the Soviet Union. The Soviets were notoriously unforgiving where Nazis were concerned and would never support Hess's release. This is one of the reasons why Britain periodically supported requests that Hess be freed; it allowed the UK to appear magnanimous and forward-thinking in victory against the petty and vindictive Soviets, safe in the knowledge that Hess would never actually win his liberty. However, Britain's bluff would be called in the mid-1980s, when the new Soviet leader Mikhail Gorbachev announced that he was lifting his state's objections to the release of Hess, saying that it 'would be accepted worldwide as a gesture of humanity'. Shortly after, Hess was found dead and another conspiracy was born.

It happened on 17 August 1987, when Spandau's last remaining inmate was discovered hanging from the window of a small summerhouse in the prison's grounds. It was said that he hung himself using the flex from a table lamp. But this story does not square with the account given by Hess's Tunisian medical orderly, Abdallah Melaouhi, who claimed that the lamp was still plugged into its socket when he arrived at the summerhouse and found his patient's lifeless body. Melaouhi also pointed out that Hess was 93 years old, suffered from severe arthritis, and could not dress himself or tie his own shoelaces, let alone hang himself. Almost immediately claims were made that Hess had been murdered. The balance of suspicion fell on Britain, whose government, it was claimed, did not want Hess to reveal sensitive information about a Nazi-backed British secret service plot to depose Winston Churchill at the height of the war. The culprits were almost certainly the two men in US Army uniforms that Melaouhi discovered at the scene and whose American accents, from the little that they said, were distinctly wobbly.

Most damning of all was the conclusion of the independent autopsy, conducted by the German forensic pathologist Dr Wolfgang Spann, which stated that Hess had died of strangulation, not by hanging. The suicide note found by Hess's body, written 'a few minutes before my death', was also debunked. It was actually shown to be a letter Hess had written some 20 years earlier, when he had been severely ill with a perforated duodenal ulcer and was about to undergo surgery that he did not think he would survive. Hess's cell was searched while he was being operated on and the note found. When he survived the operation, the note was not forwarded to Hess's family or returned to its owner. It was kept instead in his file, to resurface two decades later in convenient fashion.

Attempts by investigators to examine Hess's death scene were denied, and in any case became moot when, just days after the alleged suicide, the summerhouse in which it happened burned down. By the end of the month, Spandau Prison itself had been completely demolished. If this was not enough for those who doubted how Hess had died, the following year a book was released that blew all other conspiracy theories out of the water.

Hess: A Tale of Two Murders was written by former British Army surgeon Hugh Thomas. In 1973, he had examined Spandau's famous Nazi prisoner and came to the astonishing conclusion that he was not Rudolf Hess at all. His conclusion was based primarily on the fact that the man he examined did not have any of the bullet wounds that Hess had sustained while fighting in Romania in World War I. Thomas had released his findings in a 1979 book, named *The Murder of Rudolf Hess*, but it was his 1988 update that won the medical man a new audience. In it, he pointed out how at his trial at Nuremberg Hess had completely failed to recognize the two army secretaries he had worked with on a daily basis until his fateful flight, and how he had laughed off an attempt by an Allied officer to question him in his cell by claiming, 'Sir, there is no such person as Hess here!' (At the same time, Thomas did not devote too much attention to the fact that Hess was found to be simulating his confused and disorientated state throughout the hearing.)

Carrying on regardless, Thomas then alleged that the Messerschmitt Bf110 Hess took off in from Augsburg-Haunstetten was shot down and replaced by an identical plane piloted by Hess's double. As evidence, Thomas claimed that the code of Hess's aircraft had been NJ+C11, while that of his doppelganger was NJ+OQ. Subsequent attempts by researchers to find a Messerschmitt Bf110 in the archives with the registration NJ+C11 have so far proved fruitless. So, either Thomas's claims of a cover-up are accurate, or his theories are deluded and far-fetched.

To counter Thomas's arguments, it has been pointed out that Hess was positively identified on arrival in Scotland by Ivone Kirkpatrick, the Foreign Office's main expert on Germany. Then there are the many letters he wrote to family and friends while in captivity, which contained personal details only the real Hess would have known and whose handwriting matched that of pre-war documents he is known to have composed. But the final, fatal hole in Thomas's proposition is why would an imposter accept life imprisonment without at any point revealing their true identity?

The mystery was solved in 2019. While Hess's body had been cremated and scattered at sea to prevent his grave becoming a neo-Nazi rallying point, a blood sample taken by a US Army doctor in 1982 was found and tested. The results showed that its DNA matched that of a member of Hess's family still alive in Germany, making it 99.99 per cent certain that the man who died in Spandau, by his own hand or that of another, was Hess. The real reason why he came to be there in the first place, however, is something we will probably never know for sure.

NAZI BASE ON ANTARCTICA

In the early months of 1939, the Germans sent an expedition to the Antarctic on a ship named *Schwabenland*. It visited the western part of what is now known as Queen Maud Land, an area previously claimed by the Norwegians but which the Germans now intended to redesignate as Neuschwabenland, or New Swabia, after the region of Swabia in southern Germany.

The expedition was prompted by concerns about the future of the German whaling industry. At that time, whaling was an important activity. It supplied oil, lubricants, margarine and glycerine for the nitroglycerine used in explosives, along with other essential products.

Germany had a large investment in the industry. Its whaling fleet comprised 50 whale-catchers and seven factory ships, producing 492,532 barrels of oil in the 1938–39 whaling season. Norwegian whaling fleets had previously operated in the region, but the German government was keen not to find itself in the same situation as in the South Atlantic, where Britain asserted the right to charge heavy fees for whaling concessions and imposed restrictions on whaling activity. So it was that the *Schwabenland* found itself sailing the region's cold seas looking for a suitable base for the German whaling fleet.

The expedition was authorized by Hermann Göring as part of a German four-year plan for economic development. Its publicly avowed aim was the continuation of scientific studies Germany has begun earlier in the Weddell Sea. But it also had some secret military objectives. On its return journey, the expedition was also to investigate the suitability of using the isolated Brazilian islands of Ilha Trindade and Ilhas Martim Vaz in the Atlantic, almost 1,000 km (621 miles) off the coast of Brazil, as way stations for the German navy, particularly U-boats. Göring also wished to explore whatever strategic opportunities the Antarctic might offer. He particularly wanted to know about the functioning of aircraft at low temperatures. This knowledge would prove useful during the German invasion of the Soviet Union in 1941.

A series of expeditions was planned. The first was to map the region by air, before either making territorial claims or deciding where to locate a whaling base. The German merchantman *Schwabenland* was fitted with a catapult designed to launch a flying boat and a crane to recover it. Two follow-up expeditions in 1939–40 and 1940–41 were planned for the construction of a base once a suitable site had been found, but were apparently cancelled due to the outbreak of war.

The British, however, remained active in Antarctica during the war. Britain had laid claim to an adjoining segment of Antarctica, which included the

The MS Schwabenland *on its mission to Antarctica in 1939.*

Antarctic Peninsula and most of the surrounding islands – South Shetland, South Orkney, South Sandwich and South Georgia, which became known collectively as the Falkland Islands Dependencies. Britain had formally acquired the islands between 1908 and 1917. However, between 1925 and 1947 Argentina made claims on the same region, as did Chile in 1940.

At the start of the war, both Argentina and Chile were friendly to Germany, so Great Britain decided that it needed to demonstrate occupancy of the Falkland Islands in order to rebut competing claims from other nations. Permanently manned bases were established that could be used to monitor shipping activity and to deny the use of harbours to German ships. Meanwhile, innocent-looking support teams of researchers engaged in geographical discovery and scientific investigation.

To deny the use of the islands to Britain's enemies, HMS *Queen of Bermuda* visited Deception Island, on the west coast of the Antarctic Peninsula, in March 1941 to destroy stocks of coal and to puncture fuel tanks located there. Argentina responded by placing flags and signs on Deception Island in 1942 claiming it as their own. These were obliterated by HMS *Carnarvon Castle*, which hoisted the Union Jack there in January 1943.

Later that year, Britain began planning to occupy the territory. A secret military exercise, named Operation Tabarin, was mounted by the Royal Navy to establish bases on the peninsula and in the islands to the west. Little is known of what went on there until 10 July 1945, two months after the German surrender, when a German U-boat, *U-530*, entered the Argentine naval base at Mar del Plata. The captain of *U-530*, Lieutenant Otto Wermuth, appears to have believed that he would be well received by the Argentines. However, Argentina had broken relations with the Axis powers and joined the Allies in March 1945, so the crew of the *U-530* were interned.

The submarine's arrival created much speculation. Despite the news of Hitler's suicide on 30 April, many believed that *U-530* had somehow spirited Hitler, Eva Braun, Martin Bormann and other top Nazis out of Germany and had landed them either on the coast of Patagonia or at a mystery base referred to as 'New Berchtesgaden' in Antarctica. On 16 July, a detailed account of Hitler's supposed flight and hiding place in Queen Maud Land, Antarctica, was published in the Argentine newspaper *La Critica*, by Ladislas Szabo, a Hungarian exile.

The story was carried in major newspapers worldwide. The *Toronto Daily Star*, for example, ran it under the headline 'Hitler's on Ice in Antarctic'. Speculation increased when another German submarine, *U-977*, arrived at Mar del Plata, Argentina, on 17 August. Its commander, Oberleutnant Heinz Schaeffer, had decided at the end of the war to sail to South America rather than surrender. As with *U-530*, the crew of *U-977* was interned. Schaeffer and Wermuth were both interrogated by representatives of the Argentine Navy, the US Navy and the Royal Navy as speculation mounted that Hitler and some of his inner circle had fled Europe by submarine. No evidence was found and Wermuth, Schaeffer and their men were eventually released, but the rumours persisted.

In his 1947 book *Hitler Is Alive*, Ladislas Szabo claimed that the two submarines were part of a convoy that had taken Hitler and other senior

U-530 – *did it spirit Hitler, Eva Braun and top Nazis out of Germany?*

figures from the Third Reich to the mysterious New Berchtesgaden in Antarctica, which, he claimed, had been built during the 1939 expedition of the *Schwabenland* on the orders of Karl Dönitz, the Grand Admiral of the German Fleet. US author Jim Marrs in his 2008 book *Above Top Secret* quotes Dönitz as saying that, 'The German submarine fleet is proud of having built for the *Führer* in another part of the world a Shangri-la on land, an impregnable fortress'. The implication is that this Shangri-la was the shadowy New Berchtesgaden that many people seemed to have heard of but none had seen.

One possible location for New Berchtesgaden was in an area of Antarctica known as the Mühlig-Hofmann Mountains. These had been discovered during the 1939 *Schwabenland* expedition and were named after an official in the German Air Ministry. In one version of Hitler's last days, the story runs that the *Führer* did indeed die in his bunker and his ashes were taken by *U-977* and transported to Antarctica and deposited in what one observer called a 'very special natural ice cave in the Mühlig-Hofmann Mountains', along with other Nazi treasures, in six bronze, lead-lined boxes. It was in this geothermally-warmed 'very special natural ice cave' that a base – New Berchtesgaden – was supposedly constructed over four years from 1939.

According to James Roberts, a civil servant with the Ministry of Defence and the author of *Britain's Secret War in Antarctica*, 'In the huge cavern were underground lakes … The Nazis had constructed a huge base into the caverns and had even built docks for U-boats'. Quoting an SAS operative who claimed to have visited the site, Roberts wrote that there were 'hangars for strange planes and excavations galore had been documented … The power that the Nazis were utilizing was by volcanic activity, which gave them heat for steam and also helped produce electricity … we were overwhelmed by the numbers of personnel scurrying about like ants … huge constructions were being built … the Nazis, it appeared, had been on Antarctica a long time.'

While little physical evidence for New Berchtesgaden exists, this has not prevented the conspiracy theories surrounding it from multiplying.

Indeed, it has encouraged them: the fact that no living person can prove they have seen it is proof, the argument runs, that information about it is being suppressed.

This also goes for the secret base on Queen Maud Land that Britain allegedly operated in World War II. In *Britain's Secret War in Antarctica* James Roberts claimed that Britain used its secret installation to launch what were ultimately unsuccessful SAS attacks against Germany's secret base around Christmas 1945 (even though the SAS unit said to have carried out the raid had been disbanded months earlier). Although no official record of this raid exists, Roberts points out that a number of former SAS men on civilian 'research' and exploration contracts suddenly began to arrive in the Falkland Islands in late December 1945 and then headed off to Antarctica shortly afterwards, making for Deception Island and the military base at Port Lockroy on Wiencke Island to the west of the Antarctic Peninsula. When they returned to the Falkland Islands, at least one of the operatives had to be hospitalized in Port Stanley for unspecified reasons.

When it became clear that the SAS operation had not worked, the US launched Operation Highjump in 1946. Its commander, the polar explorer Rear-Admiral Richard E. Byrd, reportedly said that its objective was 'to break the last desperate resistance of Adolf Hitler, in case we find him in his *Neuberchtesgaden* inside New Schwabenland in the Queen Maud Land region, or to destroy him.'

In his 2004 book *Reich of the Black Sun*, US writer Joseph P. Farrell explained that, 'Outfitted for a stay of eight months, the expedition encircled the German-claimed territory of *Neuschwabenland*, Admiral Byrd stationing the naval vessels off the coast, and then advanced the ground troops and aerial reconnaissance from the pole toward the German territory. Allegedly the German "base" was quickly found, overflown, and either an American flag, or a bomb, depending on the version of the story, was dropped on the position.'

Operation Highjump was the largest expedition to Antarctica ever undertaken. It comprised just over 4,700 men, with 33 aircraft and 13 ships, including the coastguard ice-breaker *Northwind*, the aircraft carrier USS

Philippine Sea and the submarine USS *Sennet*. It was primarily a military operation, though exactly what that mission was is not entirely clear. It was 1946 and World War II was over; the Cold War had begun, and it was only natural that Operation Highjump would be seen as an anti-Soviet undertaking (which in large part it was). Its commander implied as much in an interview with the Chilean newspaper *El Mercurio* which reported that, 'Admiral Richard E. Byrd warned today that the United States should adopt measures of protection against the possibility of an invasion of the country by hostile planes coming from the polar regions. The admiral explained that he was not trying to scare anyone, but the cruel reality is that in case of a new war, the United States could be attacked by planes flying over one or both poles.'

But there are still those who argue that Operation Highjump was also a mission sent to seek and destroy the Nazis' last stronghold of New Berchtesgaden. When an American aircraft crashed during a whiteout and its crew killed it was said to have been shot down by a German secret weapon. Shortly afterwards, Operation Highjump was abruptly curtailed. In 2002's *Black Sun: Aryan Cults, Esoteric Nazism and the Politics of Identity* historian Nicholas Goodrick-Clarke discussed what this secret weapon was: UFOs. 'As early as the 1950s,' he wrote, 'rumours began to circulate among certain German nationalist circles that the post-war flying saucers were in fact German super-weapons that had been under development and tested during the Third Reich. At the time of Germany's surrender in May 1945, this technology was supposedly shipped to safety in the Arctic, South America and Antarctica. The abundance of UFO sightings was thus attributed to a hidden Nazi presence in remote and inaccessible regions of the world. By the late 1970s, neo-Nazi writers were claiming that the "Last Battalion", a massive Nazi military force of highly advanced UFOs, was in possession of a vast tract of Antarctica.'

It was said that the secret German base 'was in operation until the late 1950s, when it became the subject of an American nuclear test in which three bombs were detonated under cover of the International Geophysical Year 1957–58'. (The International Geophysical Year was a global research project

Operation Highjump – was it an attempt to destroy the Nazis' Antarctic base in 1946?

in which 67 nations conducted large-scale and often secret experiments in geology, meteorology, oceanography and other earth sciences.)

There were indeed three secret nuclear explosions in the atmosphere in the southern hemisphere in 1958, but they were not over Antarctica and they did not remain secret. They were, however, conducted by the USA as part of Operation Argus during the International Geophysical Year. But they were not intended as 'attacks' on any territory. They took place in the form that they did because they were allowed to: this was before the Nuclear Test Ban Treaty of 1963 which prohibited the testing of nuclear weapons 'in the atmosphere, in outer space, and under water'.

Operation Argus was the only clandestine series in the 17-year history of atmospheric testing. It took place 1,760 km (1,100 miles) southwest of Cape Town, South Africa, and consisted of three very high-altitude test shots of the W-25 warhead to investigate the effects of nuclear explosions outside the atmosphere, in particular how the charged particles and radioactive isotopes released would interact with the Earth's magnetic field, which could potentially interfere with radar tracking, communications, and the electronics of satellites and ballistic missiles. The tests were at heights of 160 km (100 miles), 290 km (182 miles) and 750 km (466 miles). The first took place 3,500 km (2,175 miles) north of the Queen Maud Land coast, near Tristan da Cunha, the second was 2,280 km (1,417 miles) north, and the third 2,390 km (1,485 miles) north.

The idea that there was a Nazi base on Antarctica was comprehensively discredited by scientist Colin Summerhayes and historian Peter Beeching in *Polar Record* in 2007. But that does not mean that all people will accept their findings. After all, the prospect of UFO-operating Nazis living in ice caves is too good a story to disbelieve.

COVER-UP IN THE KATYN FOREST

After Nazi Germany and the Soviet Union signed a non-aggression pact in August 1939, Hitler was free to invade Poland the following month. This marked the beginning of World War II. While Germany seized the western part of Poland, the Soviet Union seized the east. As a result, 250,000 Polish military personnel fell into Russian hands.

When Germany attacked the Soviet Union in June 1941, the government in Moscow found itself allied to Great Britain and the Polish government in exile in London. Stalin agreed to let a Polish Army be formed on Soviet territory under General Władysław Anders. One of Anders' first acts was to ask the Soviets to hand over the 15,000 Polish officers they had been holding prisoner in Smolensk to form the nucleus of his command. After an embarrassed silence, the Soviets revealed that they could not hand them over. They told Anders that, in December 1941, most of the prisoners had escaped to Manchuria and could not be located. Their whereabouts was a mystery.

However, on 13 April 1943, the Germans announced that they had discovered mass graves containing a large number of Polish officers in the Katyn Forest near Smolensk. A total of 4,443 corpses were unearthed. The victims had been shot from behind, piled in stacks and buried. Investigators determined that they were General Anders' missing officers who, the Germans said, had been executed by the Soviets in 1940.

A propaganda war ensued. The Soviets said that the Polish officers had been engaged in construction work to the west of Smolensk when the Germans arrived in August 1941 and that it was the Nazis that had killed them. But both German and Red Cross investigators were able to produce evidence that the men had been killed in 1940. When the Polish government in exile asked the International Committee of the Red Cross to produce an official report on the fate of the Polish prisoners, the Soviets refused to cooperate and, on 25 April 1943, broke off diplomatic relations with the Polish government in London. The Soviets then established a rival Polish government in exile, comprised entirely of Communists.

After the war, the Katyn massacre remained a thorn in the side of Polish–Soviet relations. The Soviet Union continued to insist that the Polish officers had been killed by the Germans and the Communist government the Russians had installed in Warsaw had no choice but to accept this. However, when a non-Communist coalition came to power in Poland in 1989, it shifted the blame to the Soviets. Finally, in April 1990, Soviet President Mikhail Gorbachev admitted that the Soviet secret police, the NKVD, was responsible for the massacre.

In the autumn of 1939, the Soviets incarcerated the Polish military prisoners they held in 138 camps. The officers were separated and imprisoned in the old Russian Orthodox monasteries at Kozelsk and Starobelsk. Each prisoner was interviewed and investigated. Those who had served as Polish intelligence operatives, military policemen, border guards and even some local policemen were segregated and transferred to the monastery at Ostashkov.

The Soviet authorities provided the prisoners with a meagre ration, just about enough to sustain them. Generals were permitted to keep their batmen, or orderlies, though. The prisoners were allowed to run their own kitchen and organize work parties to clear snow, but anyone who showed genuine leadership qualities was arrested and held incommunicado.

The Soviet State Jewellery Trust visited to buy the prisoners' watches, fountain pens and other valuables. The Poles could spend the money on additional food. Religious services were held surreptitiously. Despite everything, morale remained high.

A 1944 poster of the Katyn massacre – Nazi Germany and the Soviet Union blamed each other.

Unlike other prisoner-of-war camps, these three camps were run not by military units, but by the dreaded NKVD, the forerunner of the KGB. The men were interrogated repeatedly and attempts were made to indoctrinate them – to little effect. By March 1940, the NKVD had given up. They decided that only 448 of the 15,000 Poles they held would make suitable Communists – and these men did indeed go on to form the officer corps of the Polish Red Army after the war. Of the remaining men, some, who were German nationals, were handed over to the German authorities. That left several thousand Polish prisoners the Soviets had to decide what to do with.

The Katyn Forest lay to the west of Kozelsk. In April 1940, the men in the camp were told they were being sent home. Lists were drawn up, and those selected to go first were told to line up and return any equipment they had been given by the camp authorities. Their personal possessions were returned to them. Everything was checked carefully. The men scheduled for departure were segregated from those staying behind and were not allowed to communicate with them. They were then given a good meal, and a ration of bread and three herrings wrapped in white paper for the trip. For the men in the camp, it was heaven. White paper alone was an unimaginable luxury, never mind the food it contained.

The generals were the first to go. When they left the camp, the NKVD officers formed a guard of honour. At Starobelsk, a military band played up-tempo tunes. The other officers followed later, in groups of 50–360 men. There was no discernible pattern as to who went in which group, though officers with leadership qualities tended to be sent first. But when those who had been left behind as potential Communist recruits asked their NKVD guards why they were not being moved, they were told that they should count themselves lucky to still be in the camp.

From Ostashkov and Starobelsk, the men were taken in closed trucks to waiting trains. From Kozelsk, they were marched to the nearby railway station. The column was closely guarded by NKVD men with guns and dogs. Some Poles began to wonder why such security precautions were needed if they were really going home.

СССР

НАРОДНЫЙ КОМИССАРИАТ ВНУТРЕННИХ ДЕЛ

" марта 1940 г.
№ 794/Б

г. МОСКВА

ЦК ВКП(б)

товарищу СТАЛИНУ

В лагерях для военнопленных НКВД СССР и в тюрьмах западных областей Украины и Белоруссии в настоящее время содержится большое количество бывших офицеров польской армии, бывших работников польской полиции и разведывательных органов, членов польских националистических к-р партий, участников вскрытых к-р повстанческих организаций, перебежчиков и др. Все они являются заклятыми врагами советской власти, преисполненными ненависти к советскому строю.

Военнопленные офицеры и полицейские, находясь в лагерях, пытаются продолжать к-р работу, ведут антисоветскую агитацию. Каждый из них только и ждет освобождения, чтобы иметь возможность активно включиться в борьбу против советской власти.

Органами НКВД в западных областях Украины и Белоруссии вскрыт ряд к-р повстанческих организаций. Во всех этих к-р организациях активную руководящую роль играли бывшие офицеры бывшей польской армии, бывшие полицейские и жандармы.

Среди задержанных перебежчиков и нарушителей гос-

т. Калинин - за
Каганович - за

A memo from Beria to Stalin proposing the massacre.

At the station, they were loaded into closed prison carriages and taken to the railway station at Gnezdovo, 3 km (1.8 miles) from the Katyn graves. The first batch of 'returnees' had no idea where they were going, but the shadows cast by the telegraph poles they could glimpse through the tiny windows of their carriages told them they were going northwest – towards Poland. Those that followed found messages concerning their destination scratched into the wooden walls of the locomotive cars.

The journey took two or three days, depending on the rail traffic. When they disembarked at Gnezdovo, the men were searched. Money and valuables were confiscated. Groups of 20–30 were taken in buses into the forest. They were gagged and their arms were tied behind their backs. Ropes were looped around their necks so that, if they struggled, they would choke themselves.

The mass graves had already been dug. The Polish officers were brought six at a time and forced to kneel on the edge of the pit. Below them were layers of dead bodies, stacked neatly head to toe. Two NKVD men then walked down the line. One shot each Pole in the back of the head. The other kicked the corpse in the small of the back so that it fell into the grave. While the NKVD men went to get six more prisoners, Russian peasants standing on the corpses below pushed the fresh ones into place. This went on, hour after hour, day after day, until finally the pits were full. Then they were covered over.

It was a well-oiled killing machine run by NKVD specialists. Each prisoner was shot through the occipital bone in the back of the head, meaning that death was instantaneous.

But one Polish office taken to the Katyn Forest did manage not just to survive – he escaped, too.

His name was Lieutenant-Colonel Eugenjusz Andrei Komorowski. In September 1939, fleeing from the invading Germans, he made his way with some trepidation towards the Russian lines. He was with General Józef Olszyna-Wilczynski, the Military Commander of Grodno, who aimed to surrender to the Russians rather than the Germans. When Olszyna-Wilczynski tried to do so, he was shot by the Russians while a Polish farmer and his wife looked on and laughed.

Eventually, Komorowski ended up in the camp at Kozelsk. He was scheduled to leave on 28 April 1940. As he and his compatriots marched out of the camp they were met with a huge force of NKVD men and warned that any man trying to escape would be shot. They were subjected to a constant barrage of insults by the Russians, who considered Poles to be their inferiors.

It had rained the night before and the column had to ford a swollen stream. The banks were muddy and the men could not get a grip to stand up. As the prisoners slid around, the guards grew angry. The Poles feared that they were going to open up on them there and then. When one NKVD man lashed out with his rifle butt someone shouted: 'Kill the guards! They're planning to murder us all.' The Poles attacked the NKVD, who responded with machine gun fire. Many of the Poles were killed. Komorowski was hit in the right shoulder and right thigh. The bullets knocked him to the ground and he passed out.

When he came to, the gentle rocking motion he felt and the rhythmic clacking of metal wheels told Komorowski he was on a train. Then he caught the overwhelming smell of human excrement. Warm liquid dripped on to his face from above. Something heavy was lying on top of his body and everything around him felt soft. Before he slid back into unconsciousness, Komorowski realized he was in a train carriage filled with corpses. It was blood from the dead man he was pressed under that was dripping on to his face; the smell was that of scores of cadavers evacuating their bowels.

When Komorowski woke again it was rotting flesh he could smell this time. In the dim light he could make out the bodies of some of his friends from the camp. His right shoulder and thigh burned with pain. He was sure he had broken bones. He prayed that none of his vital organs had been hit. Afraid that he was going to die, Komorowski's thoughts turned to his wife and to all the other beautiful women he had known.

The train came to a stop. He heard voices outside and doors creaking open. Men were being ordered to get on to buses. Then, the door on his compartment opened.

'Drag the bastards out,' a voice said. 'The truck is coming.'

Komorowski played dead. As they lifted him out, two Russians discussed whether to steal his smart Polish Army boots.

'Do you want to be shot?' one of them said. 'They're to be buried in Katyn with boots and papers so that no trace of them will ever be found.'

Outside it was cold. They dragged Komorowski's body like a rag doll and lay him on the ground. After a while a truck arrived and the corpses were flung on to it. Komorowski counted 14 thuds as they landed. Luckily, he was the last.

The truck bumped up a hill and through a gate. Komorowski saw barbed wire and began to shiver in the cold air. Somehow, he managed to get the trembling under control by the time they reached a wooden lodge. Beyond it he saw a group of Polish officers. The truck slowed. An NKVD officer examined the corpses and directed the truck to the right, deeper into the forest.

It came to a halt by a mass grave and Komorowski could see Russian peasants walking on the corpses. There were more bodies than he could count. He lay still and watched while his brother officers were murdered and saw how they were stacked so that the grave would hold the maximum number of bodies. Weak from loss of blood and the horror of what had happened to him, Komorowski could not fully take in what he saw. Suddenly, a wave of nausea swept over him.

He closed his eyes and tried to block out what he had seen. He struggled to keep the smell of rotting flesh out of his nostrils. The grave must had been open for days. Somehow, he resisted vomiting. Somehow, he resisted screaming. Somehow, he resisted weeping. He lay there silently until the NKVD mass murderers had finished their day's work. Then the peasants came to unload the truck. Komorowski was lucky again. He was thrown face down on top of the last man to be killed. His body was still warm. And no one was put on top of him.

It was late and the peasants decided to cover the corpses with earth the next day. The Russians drove off and the forest fell silent. Komorowski lay there on top of layer upon layer of his dead comrades and wept.

A cold wind ruffled the back of his hair. Gingerly, he raised his head.

Then he realized that he no longer had to play dead. Everybody living had gone.

He thought of his wife again. In his imagination, she told him to muster all of his strength and get out of there before the Russians came back. He pulled himself out of the grave and stumbled towards some trees. He looked for the North Star. He surmised that the train station was to the south, so he headed north. He would clear the area and then turn west for Poland.

Progress was slow. He was in considerable pain. In the darkness, with tears in his eyes, he kept bumping into trees. But every so often, after finding a clearing, he would check the position of the North Star and continue his halting journey.

Eventually, he reached a river and waded through its freezing water. Cold, hungry and weak from loss of sleep, he kept blacking out. Eventually, he snagged his coat on a barbed wire fence. He cut his hands trying to free himself and eventually gave up and fell asleep. When he awoke, there was a fog. He climbed the fence. When he looked back the fog was lifting and he could see peasants turning up for work at a lodge. This spurred him on.

His situation seemed hopeless. But in his pocket he found a bar of chocolate and a can of herring he had bought from the camp shop after selling his watch. He ate the chocolate, then smashed the tin open with a rock. Oil splashed on to some leaves, so Komorowski picked them up and licked it off. The food gave him renewed strength and he hobbled on.

The sun came out and dried his clothes. It also helped him navigate. He reached a barn, where he washed his wounds in a pail of water. He was lucky. The two bullets that had hit him had passed right through his body. He drank some milk direct from the teat of a cow and found an old smock and some baggy trousers which he changed into.

Out in the forest again, he made a fire and burned his uniform and papers. He buried his boots. He travelled on, barefoot, foraging for food. A few days later, he stole an old pair of boots from a barn.

Avoiding houses, he crept into barns at night to sleep. But soon he realized that he would need other people's help if he were to survive. One evening, he climbed up on to the porch of a remote house and begged the people inside for assistance. Eventually, they let him in, fed him, tended his wounds and said they would let him sleep in the loft for one night. But once he had gone to sleep, they went to fetch the police. Luckily for Komorowski, he was a light sleeper. He heard the man of the house saddle his horse and managed to escape.

He made his way across Russia, stealing food wherever he could. Then, one day, he heard people speaking Polish. He was back in Poland. But that was not the end of his troubles. If he stopped and asked people for help, he could endanger their lives. And there was always a possibility that the people he spoke to would be Russian Poles whose sympathies were with the occupying forces.

Eventually, he reached the farmhouse where General Olszyna-Wilczynski had been shot and went in to see the couple who had ingratiated themselves with the Russians by laughing at the general's execution. They were not pleased to see him. There was a violent row and Komorowski killed them both. He felt no remorse and left the bodies on the kitchen floor as he helped himself to their food. Then he blew out the light and went to bed.

In the morning, he stole the man's papers and a suit and headed to Grodno. When he presented the papers at the sentry post outside town, he distracted the guard with a few words of Russian. Then came the worst shock of all. When he reached home, he found another couple living in his apartment. They told him his wife had been shot by the Russians. The grief drove him temporarily insane. Then he wanted revenge. He resolved to leave Poland and carry on fighting – and tell the world what had happened at Katyn.

He made his way to Romania, with the idea of travelling on to Paris. But the French capital had already fallen to the Germans by then, so he decided to go to Switzerland instead. He crossed Hungary and Czechoslovakia by hoboing on trains. In his numbed mental state, he took incredible risks. His lack of fear seemed to help him. He rode freight trains across Austria, then walked across the border into Switzerland. There, he gave himself up to a policeman who took him to the Red Cross. They fed and washed him and informed the Polish authorities. When two Polish officers arrived, they did not believe that he had come all the way from Russia, preferring to suppose that he had escaped from a German camp. They flew him to London. By then, Komorowski's mind had erased all memory of the horrors of the Katyn Forest. It was years before the full truth of the atrocity he had witnessed came back to him.

But a mystery still remains. The Germans only found 4,443 bodies in the mass graves at Katyn, all of them from the camp at Kozelsk. What had happened to the other 10,000 or so who had been at Ostashkov and Starobelsk? Some witnesses say that at least 6,000 of them were taken to Archangel and put on barges, which were floated out in to the White Sea. The barges were then sunk by artillery fire and the men drowned in the freezing water.

An NKVD document dated 10 June 1940 indicates they were murdered and buried in mass graves at Bologyne and Dergachi in Ukraine. In 1991, a mass grave was found at Piatikhatki, near Kharkiv, which was thought to contain the bodies of the men from Starobelsk. But the KGB only allowed the exhumation of 140 bodies there. So, it is still not known where the rest of

A memorial to the victims of the Katyn massacre.

the Polish officers are buried. In fact, no one knows where the bodies buried in Katyn are. Once the Soviets regained the territory from the Germans later in the war, they set about trying to remove all trace of the massacre. In 1944, Soviet earth-moving machines were photographed digging at Katyn. They were removing the bodies and destroying the graves. Although the bodies are gone, Katyn is where the memorial to all 15,000 missing Polish officers stands.

But why did the Soviets slaughter these men in the first place? Like the Germans, the Soviets wanted to control Poland. Once they discovered that they had virtually all of Poland's senior military men in their hands, the Soviets set about first trying to convert them to their ideological cause and then, where that failed, eliminating the men who were trained to be their country's future leaders and administrators. With them gone, the Soviets knew they would be free to put their own proxies in power once the war was over – which is exactly what they did until the fall of Communism in 1989. In the meantime, this also allowed them to cover up the events at Katyn for more than 40 years.

CONSPIRACY TO COUNTERFEIT

During the war, Nazi Germany forged British currency – then a reserve currency used for international trade – in an attempt to destabilize the UK economy. The idea was put forward by *SS-Gruppenführer* Arthur Nebe, the head of the *Reichskriminalpolizeiamt* – the central criminal investigation department of Nazi Germany. Some £30 billion in forged notes were to be dropped over Britain. While honest people would presumably hand in most of them, it was thought that enough would be retained and spent to cause runaway inflation.

At a meeting on 18 September 1939 to discuss the matter, Walther Funk, the Reich Minister for Economic Affairs, objected to the plan on the grounds that it would breach international law. But as Britain and Germany were at war, this was not a concern that bothered Hitler. The counterfeiting plot was called *Unternehmen Andreas* ('Operation Andreas').

Two months later, a Russian émigré gave full details of the plot to the British ambassador in Greece, who informed London. The Bank of England and the US Department of the Treasury were alerted. The Bank released an emergency £1 note with a metal security thread running through the paper. This may have been an overreaction; the first counterfeit notes were not detected until 1943, when one came over the counter of a bank in Tangiers.

In Britain, the importation of sterling was banned. No new notes of £10 or above were released and a new £5 note was issued. It was blue and printed on both sides, rather than the old 'white fiver' which had black printing on only one side of the white note.

In early 1940, a counterfeiting unit was set up in Berlin in the technical department of the *Sicherheitsdienst* (*SD*), headed by *SS-Sturmbannführer* Alfred Naujocks and run by Albert Langer, a mathematician and codebreaker. They decided to concentrate on the £5 note first as there were more of them in circulation.

Samples of genuine £5 notes were analysed and attempts were made to replicate the rag paper used. There were problems matching the colour at first. When that was achieved, they found that the replica differed from the original under ultraviolet light. The problem was the chemical balance of the water used to soak the paper pulp and cloth, so efforts were made to duplicate the chemistry of British water.

Next, the forgers had to work out the alphanumeric sequence of the serial numbers of the notes. Here, Langer's cryptographic skills came into play. Then they had problems with the intricate vignette of Britannia represented on the notes, particularly the eyes. But when this was achieved, Naujocks fell out with *SD* boss Reinhard Heydrich and was sent to the Eastern Front. Langer also left in early 1942 and the operation was closed down. It had produced around £3 million in forged notes. But few were ever distributed. The Luftwaffe could not spare the planes to drop them.

The plan was revived in July 1942 under *SS-Sturmbannführer* Bernhard Krüger, as Operation Bernhard. This time the forged currency was not to be used to destabilize the British economy, but rather to finance German foreign intelligence operations. And instead of using forgers culled from German police files, they would use inmates from concentration camps.

A new counterfeiting unit was set up in the compound at Sachsenhausen, 32 km (20 miles) north of Berlin. Krüger searched other concentration camps for inmates with skills in draughtsmanship, engraving, printing and banking. Eighty were assembled. They were treated well and given special privileges. Paper and ink arrived. Printing began in January 1943.

But mid-1943 they were producing 65,000 notes a month from six flat-bed printing presses running 24 hours a day. The workforce was increased to 140, working in two 12-hour shifts. Between 40 to 50 prisoners stood in two columns, passing the notes back and forth so that they accumulated dirt, sweat and general wear and tear in order to appear used. Some prisoners would fold and refold the notes; others would make pin holes in the corners to replicate how a teller would attach a paper note to a bundle. Numbers

A forged £5 note – part of an attempt to ruin the British economy.

were also written on some notes, the way a bank clerk would mark the value of a wad. British names and addresses were sometimes written on the reverse, the way British people used to do. The Nazis were so pleased with the results that 12 prisoners were awarded the War Merit Medal. Three of them were Jewish.

By late 1943, approximately one million notes per month were being printed. They were transferred from SS headquarters to a former hotel near Merano in Trentino-Alto Adige, northern Italy. From there, the money was laundered and used to purchase strategic imports and to pay German agents. Turkish agent Elyesa Bazna – codenamed Cicero – was paid in counterfeit notes for obtaining secrets from the British embassy in Ankara. It has been reported that counterfeit currency was used to obtain information that helped to free the Italian leader Benito Mussolini in the Gran Sasso raid of September 1943.

The money laundering operation was run by smuggler Friedrich Schwend, who had been handling illegal currency since the 1930s. He ran a network of 50 agents and subagents, each of whom received their cut. Some of them were Jewish, as they would not be suspected of working for the Nazis.

The counterfeiting team then turned its attention to US dollars. But this was in late 1944–early 1945, and by then it was becoming clear which way the war was turning. Although sample $100 bills were ready by 22 February 1945, the Reich Security Main Office decided that they would no longer be needed. Production at Sachsenhausen was slowed down and then halted.

The counterfeiting team and their machinery were transferred to Redl-Zipf in Austria, a subsidiary of the Mauthausen-Gusen concentration camp. An order to restart the operation in the tunnels beneath the camp was soon rescinded.

At the beginning of May 1945, Operation Bernhard was closed down completely and the counterfeiting team was sent to the Ebensee concentration camp. An order was given that they were to be killed together once they had arrived, but their SS guards had only one truck and the transfer required three round trips. The truck broke down during the third trip and the last batch of prisoners had to be marched to Ebensee, a journey that took two days. By then, most of the guards at Ebensee had fled. The inmates revolted against the remaining soldiers and refused to be moved into tunnels under the camp which were to have been blown up. The counterfeiters who had already been delivered to Ebensee dispersed themselves among the camp's other inmates, making them difficult to identify. When the third batch of counterfeiters at long last arrived, their guards were not able to sequester them with the other forgers. As the orders had been to execute all of the counterfeiters together, the guards could not act. This action by the camp's prisoners saved them all. None of the counterfeiters died at Ebensee.

The Ebensee camp was liberated by US forces on 6 May 1945. After the war, Major Krüger was detained by the British for two years, then turned over to the French for another 12 months. In the end, Krüger faced no

Survivors from the Ebensee concentration camp where the forgers ended up.

charges as counterfeiting was not a war crime. He was released in 1948. In the 1950s, Krüger went before a De-Nazification Court, where statements were read from the forger-inmates whose lives he had saved. He later worked for the company which had produced the special paper for the Operation Bernhard forgeries. He died in 1989.

The smuggler Friedrich Schwend amassed a fortune from Operation Bernhard. He was captured by American forces in June 1945 and handed over to the Gehlen Organization, the German intelligence agency set up by US forces in occupied Germany. After he was caught trying to defraud the network, Schwend fled to Peru. Although he acted as an informant for Peruvian intelligence, he was arrested for currency smuggling and selling state secrets. After a two-year prison sentence, Schwend was deported to West Germany where, in 1979, he was tried for a wartime murder. This was reduced to manslaughter and he was given a suspended sentence.

Estimates of the number and value of notes printed during Operation Bernhard vary from a total of £132,610,945 up to £300 million. Most of the notes were thought to have ended up at the bottom of Lake Toplitz near Ebensee, from where some were recovered by divers in 1959. Nevertheless, examples continued to turn up in circulation in Britain for many years. It was not until the early 1960s that £10 notes were reintroduced in the UK; £20s followed in 1970 and £50s in 1980.

SETTING FIRE TO EUROPE

On 13 June 1940, Britain's newly appointed prime minister, Winston Churchill, set up a secret organization to, 'coordinate all action by way of sabotage and subversion against the enemy overseas'. It was called the Special Operations Executive (SOE). To conceal its existence, its various departments were given innocuous names such as the 'Joint Technical Board' or the 'Inter-Service Research Bureau', or were designated as fictitious branches of the Air Ministry, Admiralty or War Office.

Those in the know called it 'Churchill's Secret Army', 'the Ministry of Ungentlemanly Warfare' or the 'Baker Street Irregulars' (its London HQ was at 64 Baker Street). This last name was also that of the gang of street boys employed by Sherlock Holmes in Sir Arthur Conan Doyle's detective stories.

Churchill told his first Minister of Economic Warfare, Hugh Dalton, nominally the politician overseeing the SOE, that its job was to 'go and set Europe ablaze'. The director of operations was a Commando, Brigadier Colin Gubbins. He had been involved in planning to establish a sabotage force to work behind the lines if Germany had succeeded in invading Britain. At the SOE, his plans included blowing up trains, bridges and factories, as well as fomenting revolt and guerrilla warfare in enemy-occupied countries.

Though its senior members were army officers, the SOE was run independently of the military and of the Secret Intelligence Service (SIS, which was designated as MI6 in wartime), which also operated abroad and in occupied countries. It maintained its own training, research and development, and administrative centres, often in country houses. The joke was that SOE stood for 'Stately 'Omes of England'.

The department for the development of devices to be used in irregular warfare, codenamed MD1, was located at The Firs in Whitchurch, Buckinghamshire. It was nicknamed 'Churchill's Toyshop' because the prime minister took a particular interest in the weird and wonderful weapons they came up with. Another bureau, Station IX, also developed weapons, explosive devices, booby traps and portable radio transmitters at The Frythe, a former hotel outside Welwyn Garden City. The Welrod, a pistol with built-in silencer, and the sleeve gun, a single-shot version that could be hidden up a sleeve, were both developed there.

Station XV, at the Thatched Barn near Borehamwood, was devoted to camouflage, devising ways of hiding weapons, explosives or radios in everyday items. It also equipped agents with local clothing and personal effects.

At Briggens House near Roydon in Essex, Station XIV produced identity papers, ration cards, currency and other documentation for agents. As the SOE's central forgery department, it employed a number of ex-convicts, mainly skilled counterfeiters.

Unarmed combat and the art of silent killing were taught at Wanborough Manor near Guildford in Surrey, where recruits were also briefed on the current situation in France and the other occupied countries where they would be operating. As well as language lessons, firearms handling, sabotage, explosives training, map reading and communications using Morse code were also taught.

For those who passed the four-week course at Wanborough, further training with arms and explosives took place at Arisaig House in Inverness-shire. Agents requiring further training – such as radio operators or demolition experts – went on to other specialist establishments. Security and spy craft were taught at schools around Beaulieu in Hampshire. Lastly, recruits were given parachute training prior to infiltration.

Agents were armed with handguns and fighting knives, including small ones that could be hidden behind a lapel or in the heel of a shoe. They

A demolition class of the SOE at Milton Hall in 1944.

were also trained in the use of enemy weapons. And, given the grisly fate that awaited them if they were captured, they were issued with suicide pills.

The SOE developed a wide range of explosive devices for sabotage, such as limpet mines, shaped charges and time fuses, which were also widely used by Commando units. The time pencil, where acid ate through a retaining wire in a spring-loaded detonator, gave the agent time to escape before the explosion.

Plastic explosives were pioneered by the SOE. These could be shaped or cut in situ and could be transported safely as they required a powerful detonator to set them off. Plastic explosives were used in everything from car bombs to exploding rats designed to destroy coal-fired boilers (this required an unusual form of taxidermy, where dead rats were gutted and filled with explosives. The idea was to leave them close to boilers, so that when the corpses were discovered they would be picked up and thrown into the fiery furnaces by their unsuspecting operators). Explosives concealed in coal piles were also used to destroy locomotives and land mines were disguised as cow pats. Another sabotage technique widely used was the introduction of abrasive materials into the oil used to lubricate axles or gearboxes.

The medieval caltrop, a small, cross-shaped metal device with sharpened spikes, was revived by the SOE to burst tyres or injure the feet of soldiers. Elastic band-powered folding crossbows were developed that fired incendiary bolts. Station IX developed a miniature folding motorbike, too, along with exploding pens and guns concealed in tobacco pipes – though there is no evidence of them being used.

When Air Marshal Arthur 'Bomber' Harris objected to his planes being diverted from bombing raids in order to drop agents and equipment over enemy territory, SOE got its own aircraft. These were also used to pick up agents from makeshift airfields when an operation was completed. They flew from RAF Tempsford in Bedfordshire and RAF Tangmere, close to the coast in West Sussex.

Some operatives carried Rebecca/Eureka transponding radar, so that planes could locate them on the ground. The SOE also developed the S-Phone, a two-way UHF radio that allowed agents on the ground to communicate with aircraft in flight.

While the Royal Navy could in theory deliver agents by submarine, leaving them to paddle ashore in a dinghy or canoe, it was felt that submersibles were too valuable to use – and potentially lose – so close to shore. Instead, fishing boats and skiffs that could pass as local vessels were used to deliver SOE operatives and their kit to mission sites. The SOE also recruited Norwegian seamen and fishermen, who had fled when the Nazis invaded, to run the 'Shetland Bus', a clandestine service carrying agents in and out of Scandinavia. Later, the SOE acquired its own fleet of fast motorboats.

One of the SOE's most famous operations was the assassination of *SS-Obergruppenführer* Reinhard Heydrich, Himmler's deputy and one of the architects of the Holocaust. In September 1941, Heydrich was made

Reichsprotektor – 'governor' – of Bohemia and Moravia in modern Czechia, to suppress resistance in the occupied territory. Anyone who did not collaborate was shot or sent to a concentration camp. The very definition of a hard taskmaster, Heydrich issued ration cards to armament factory workers based on their output. Not surprisingly, industrial productivity in Bohemia and Moravia went up. The British government feared that this would encourage collaboration in other occupied territories. It had to be stopped.

The SOE devised Operation Anthropoid and 200 exiled Czechoslovakian soldiers were sent to one of the SOE's Commando training camps in Scotland to train for it. Though assassination was generally disapproved of in the military, two of the exiles – Jan Kubiš, a Czech, and Jozef Gabčík, a Slovak – were selected to be dropped in Czechoslovakia and kill Heydrich. After landing safely, they made their way to a safe house in Prague where they planned their attack.

At 10.30 am on 27 May 1942, Heydrich set off on his daily commute from his home in Panenské Břežany, 15 km (9 miles) north of the city, to his headquarters at Prague Castle. He rode in a green, open-topped Mercedes 320 Cabriolet B, driven by *SS-Oberscharführer* Hans Klein. Gabčík and Kubiš waited at a tram stop along the route where a tight curve would force the car to slow down. Another member of the party, Josef Valčík, was stationed around 90 m (300 ft) ahead to act as a lookout.

As Heydrich's car approached, Gabčík stepped into the road and opened fire with a Sten gun. Heydrich ordered Klein to stop the car and stood up to return fire. Kubiš then threw a briefcase containing a modified anti-tank grenade, possibly carrying a biological agent, at the rear of the car. It detonated, ripping through the rear bumper and peppering Heydrich with shrapnel and fibres from the shredded upholstery. Kubiš was also injured, but, along with Gabčík, continued shooting at the wounded Heydrich as he stepped out the car. Stunned by the explosion, they missed.

Kubiš jumped on a bicycle to make his escape. Heydrich ran after him but collapsed from shock. He ordered Klein to chase after Gabčík. Klein cornered his quarry in a butcher's, but Gabčík shot him twice and wounded him in the leg. Gabčík then jumped on a tram and the two assassins returned to their safe house.

Heydrich was rushed to hospital, but died a week later. Hitler ordered reprisals and declared that 10,000 Czechs be executed, but Himmler warned that indiscriminate killings might damage productivity. Nevertheless, there were mass arrests, including friends and family of the assassins. Kubiš's girlfriend, Anna Malinová, was seized. She died in the Mauthausen-Gusen concentration camp five months later. But still the assassins had not been caught.

A Gestapo report suggested they were hiding in the village of Lidice. Hitler ordered its complete destruction. Its population of 199 men were killed and its 195 women were deported to the Ravensbrück concentration camp. Of the 95 children taken prisoner, 81 were later killed in gas vans at the Chełmno extermination camp, while eight were adopted by German families. The village of Ležáky was also destroyed, because a radio

Jan Kubiš and Jozef Gabčík, the assassins who killed Heydrich.

transmitter had been found there. Its population was murdered. Both villages were burned and the ruins of Lidice were levelled.

Further reprisals were threatened if the assassins had not been caught by 18 June. The safe house where the assassins had taken refuge was betrayed for a bounty of one million Reichsmarks. It belonged to the Moravec family. When it was raided on 17 June, Marie Moravec killed herself with a cyanide tablet.

Her husband, Alois Moravec, was unaware of his wife's involvement with the Resistance. He was tortured along with his 17-year-old son Ata, who refused to talk until he was shown his mother's severed head in a fish tank and warned that his father's would be next. Ata, who like his mother was a Resistance operative, revealed that Gabčík and Kubiš had moved on to the Karel Boromejsky Church. Ata Moravec was executed by the Nazis in Mauthausen on 24 October 1942, on the same day as his father, along with Ata's fiancée, her mother and her brother.

Some 750 Waffen-SS troops surrounded the church. They tried to flush out the assassins with tear gas. When that failed, they called in fire trucks to flood the basement. Gabčík and Kubiš, and five other supporters with them in the crypt, died in the furious gun battle that ensued or by suicide.

Two years later, Operation Foxley, a plan to assassinate Hitler, was drawn up but not implemented. It was thought that Hitler's incompetent interference in military strategy, particularly on the Eastern Front, was working in favour of the Allies and rendered his death unnecessary.

However, Operation Periwig did go ahead. This aimed to create the illusion that there was a growing Resistance movement in Germany. Weapons, ammunition, propaganda material and supplies were dropped by aeroplane and radio messages were sent to imaginary cells. German prisoners of war were trained and dropped behind the lines to liaise with the Resistance (not knowing that it did not exist). This meant that if any of them betrayed their mission and reported to the authorities, it would only enhance the illusion that there was an opposition network operating in the Reich.

Propaganda material using the symbol of a red horse was disseminated. The ostensible aim of the Red Horse Movement was to execute high-ranking

Nazi functionaries. Letters carrying the red horse symbol were sent to targets, causing security around them to be tightened, taking up scarce manpower and fostering paranoia. The red horse symbol also appeared on the sides of buildings. No such Red Horse Movement actually existed.

Pigeons carrying capsules containing questionnaires and pencils were dropped behind enemy lines, inviting people to return details of troop movements. In fact, only nine out of the 330 capsules dropped were returned to England. Only five contained return messages and only one provided any useful information. In many respects, this didn't matter; the activity served a more useful purpose in encouraging the idea that there was an anti-Nazi conspiracy afoot.

But there were failures. The SOE network in the Netherlands was compromised and 50 agents rounded up. Only two escaped. Cooperation between the SOE and the Polish Home Army delivered the first Allied intelligence on the Holocaust to London in June 1942. Although plans were drawn up to liberate the inmates of Auschwitz, they were rejected as unfeasible.

The SOE supported local French Resistance groups in sabotage operations, crucially in France before the D-Day landings with Operation Jedburgh, conducted jointly with the American Office of Strategic Services (OSS). Agents were parachuted into France immediately before the landings and in the months afterwards. Three-man teams led local French Resistance forces in actions that delayed German columns reaching the fighting in Normandy.

A typical SOE agent was Michael Trotobas. Half French, he was recruited to the SOE's French Section after escaping from Dunkirk and given a commission in the Manchester Regiment. In 1941, he was parachuted into the Chateauroux area in central France under the codename 'Sylvestre'. Six weeks later, he was arrested with nine other agents. However, the following year, he took part in a mass escape from Mauzac Prison, going on to establish and lead the Lille-based 'Farmer' Resistance circuit.

From 1943, Trotobas successfully led a sabotage campaign, targeting the Lans-Béthune railway, tool factories at Armentières, and naval depots at Boulogne and Calais. In June 1943, his group damaged the Lilles-Fives locomotive works.

Trotobas was killed in November 1943, while trying to evade arrest after the Germans extracted the address of his safe house from a captured agent. He was recommended for a posthumous Victoria Cross, but this was rejected as no senior officer had been present to witness his bravery. This was a common outcome for special-forces personnel.

Women agents played a crucial role in special operations. One of the most famous was Violette Szabo. She had a French mother and an English father, and grew up in London. Following the death of her French husband

Violette Szabo, who was executed in Ravensbrück concetration camp.

at the Battle of El Alamein in 1942, she joined the Auxiliary Territorial Service. Her French background made her an ideal recruit for the SOE's French Section, and she was enlisted in the all-woman First Aid Nursing Yeomanry, or FANY, as cover.

After training, Violette was parachuted into occupied France with her suitcase transmitter and fake papers, joining the 'Salesman' circuit in April 1944. When this group was exposed, she was forced to return to Britain by plane.

She returned to France after the D-Day landings, parachuting into Limoges on 8 June 1944. She assisted the Resistance in sabotaging German lines of communication. This included helping delay the deployment of the 2nd SS Panzer Division *Das Reich* from the south of France to Normandy. Agents siphoned axle oil from the division's rail transport cars, replacing it with abrasive grease that seized them up.

Violette was captured on 10 June. Following her interrogation and torture she was sent to Ravensbrück concentration camp and executed in February 1945. In December 1947, her five-year-old daughter Tania received the George Cross from King George VI on behalf of her mother.

In 1943, SOE parachutists also took part in the destruction of the heavy water plant at Vemork in Norway, which delayed the Nazis' atomic bomb programme. During the subsequent campaign in Belgium and Holland, the teams continued to provide an essential link between Resistance groups and the Allied command.

The SOE also operated in eastern Europe, Africa and Southeast Asia. The British government considered some of its activities unlawful and it was disbanded in 1946. Some of the personnel were taken on by MI6. Consequently, the exploits of this secret army remained secret for many years after the war.

BLACK PROPAGANDA

The Political Warfare Executive (PWE) grew out of the Special Operations Executive. Its primary aim was the dissemination of black propaganda to undermine the enemy's morale. It was formed in August 1941, mainly with staff from the SOE's propaganda department. The chairman was Robert Bruce Lockhart, a British diplomat who had been behind a plot to assassinate Lenin in Russia in 1918.

The mastermind behind its black propaganda operations was the journalist Sefton Delmer. He had been born in Berlin to Australian parents and his father was Professor of English Literature at Berlin University. The family was interned on the outbreak of World War I and repatriated to Britain in 1917 in a prisoner exchange. Delmer had spoken only German until the age of five and was educated in a German gymnasium, leaving him with an accent.

After graduating in German from Lincoln College, Oxford, he worked as a freelance journalist before being hired by the *Daily Express* and sent back to Berlin as its bureau chief. He attended a Nazi meeting in Berlin in 1929, where Hitler exhorted the audience not to eat foreign fruit such as oranges, and dismissed the Party leader as a crackpot.

He later became friends with Ernst Röhm, who arranged for him to become the first British journalist to interview Hitler. He travelled with Hitler on his private plane during the 1932 election campaign and became so close with the would-be *Führer* that the Nazis thought he was a British spy, while the British believed he was in the pay of the Nazi Party. Delmer famously accompanied Hitler when he walked through the smouldering ruins of the Reichstag in February 1933.

Later that year, Delmer was transferred to his newspaper's Paris bureau and then went to cover the Spanish Civil War. At the outbreak of World War II he was in Poland, before returning to London where he went to work for the BBC German-language service. When Hitler offered peace terms in a broadcast on 19 July 1940, Delmer responded immediately, without authority, that Britain hurled the terms 'right back at you, in your evil-smelling teeth'. The Germans assumed that the BBC could not have responded in such a way without the sanction of Winston Churchill.

Delmer was recruited by the SOE and then moved to the PWE, where he dedicated himself to sabotaging the German war effort by spreading rumours and false reports. The PWE set up the radio station *Gustav Siegfried Eins*, the phonetic rendering of *GP1* – which the listener could have taken for *Geheimsender 1* ('Secret Transmitter 1') or *Generalstab 1* ('General Staff 1'). This was run ostensibly by *Der Chef* ('the boss'), supposedly a Prussian officer of the old school who looked down on the Nazis. Its aim was to undermine confidence in Germany's Nazi leaders among the ordinary people by criticizing their actions and presenting the armed forces as an alternative source of state authority to the Nazis. The 'boss' in fact was Peter Seckelmann, a German detective novelist recruited by Delmer to play the role of the crotchety military man. An unimpeachable anti-Nazi, Seckelmann's father had committed suicide after the Nazis came to power in 1933; his mother would be murdered in the Theresienstadt ghetto in 1943.

The radio station began broadcasting to German audiences in May 1941, just after Rudolf Hess had flown to Scotland. The boss informed his listeners that, 'This rascal is by far not the worst. In the days of the *Freikorps* he stood his ground. But just like this whole clique of bunglers, megalomaniacs, masterminds and Salon Bolsheviks who are at the head of our government, he has nerves of steel that are far too weak to endure a crisis. As soon as he learns something of the darker side of what is to come – what does he do? He completely loses his head, packs a few boxes

„Es gibt kein Zurück!"

—ALFRED ROSENBERG AM 25. VIII. 1941

DER WEG DER PIMPFE

ACHT Jahre ist es her, seit die zwölfjährigen Hitlerpimpfe auf dem ersten Parteitag in Nürnberg mitmarschieren durften. Für die Buben war es herrlich, dieses Kriegspielen. Sie verstanden nichts von Politik, und sie konnten ja nicht ahnen, für welchen bitteren Ernstfall dieses Spiel sie vorbereitete.

Die Pimpfe von damals sind es, die heute zu Hunderttausenden in Russland fallen. Eine ganze Generation deutscher Jugend wird für den Welteroberungswahn ihres Führerklüngels hingeschlachtet.

Es ist zu spät, diese Jahrgänge zu retten. Erst acht Jahre lang geistig und seelisch verdorben, dann von einem unfehlbaren Führer zum Sterben abkommandiert — sie sind verloren.

Eine neue Generation wächst in Deutschland heran. Auch sie lernt Krieg spielen. Auch sie wird mit kalt berechnender Gründlichkeit herangebildet für „den erhabensten Augenblick im Leben des deutschen Menschen".

Die Hitlerpimpfe von 1933 liegen in den Massengräbern in russischer Erde oder in Lazaretten fern von der Heimat. Die Hitlerpimpfe von 1941 sind noch immer Pimpfe, schuldlos und lebensfroh. Sind auch sie verdammt, den Weg ihrer Brüder zu gehen?

1933

„Parteitag des Sieges"

Sie spielten Krieg in Nürnberg—

1941

†

in Russland

Hitlers und Churchills Kriegsziele

Alfred Rosenberg am 25. August 1941:

„Sinn und Ziel unseres Kampfes ist ein germanisches Europa . . . . Und sollte jemand fragen, welche Vorbereitungen Adolf Hitler für einen Rückzug getroffen hat, dann wird jeder von uns antworten: Deutsches Volk, es gibt kein Zurück! Es geht um Grossdeutschland !"

Winston Churchill am 24. August 1941:

„Zwischen der Haltung, welche die Vereinigten Staaten und Grossbritannien heute einnehmen, und zwischen der, welche die Alliierten im letzten Abschnitt des vorigen Weltkrieges eingenommen haben, bestehen zwei deutliche Unterschiede. Erstens: die Vereinigten Staaten und Grossbritannien sind heute nicht mehr der Ansicht, dass es von selbst nie wieder zu einem Krieg kommen werde. Im Gegenteil, wir wollen weitgehende Vorsichtsmassnahmen treffen, um seine Wiederholung zu verhindern, indem wir die schuldigen Nationen wirksam entwaffnen, während wir selbst uns angemessen geschützt bleiben.

Zweitens: anstatt dass wir versuchen — wie es im Jahr 1917 gang und gäbe war — den deutschen Handel durch allerlei zusätzliche Handelsschranken zu unterbinden, haben wir uns die Ansicht zu eigen gemacht, dass es nicht im Interesse der Welt und unserer Länder liegt, eine grosse Nation vom Wohlstand auszuschliessen. Diese Leitsätze umreissen einen grundlegenden Wechsel unserer Einstellung über jede frühere nachkehren sollte."

GEFALLEN

Zweieinhalb Millionen deutsche Soldaten sind, nach amtlichen russischen Berichten, bisher an der Ostfront getötet oder verwundet worden. Hier ist eine kurze Liste west- und süddeutscher Provinzen und Länder, die besonders schwer gelitten haben:

Westfalen-Nord (Münster): 16.Infanterieregiment, 453. und 464. Infanterieregiment.

Köln-Aachen: 26. Infanterie-Division.

Mannheim: motorisierte Division.

Hessen-Nassau: Infanterieregiment.

Kurhessen: Division.

Franken: motorisierte Division.

Main-Franken: Panzer-Division.

Württemberg: und 15. Infanterieregiment.

GESTIEGEN

Seit Beginn des russischen Feldzugs sind die Rüstungswerte an der Berliner Börse stark gestiegen. Hier sind einige Beispiele:

	Aktienkurse	
	am 21.6.41	9 Wochen später
Conti-Gummi	375	426½
Daimler-Benz	195	215
Deutsche Waffen	296	314
Dynamit Nobel	109	138½
Grün & Bilfinger	401	480
Heinrich Lanz	242	298½
Rheinische Braunkohle	296	342
Siemens & Halske	318½	352
Vereinigte Deutsche Nickel	247	293½
Zeiss Ikon	216	259½

of hormone pills and a white flag in his briefcase, and flies off to the mercy of himself and us to that flat-footed bastard of a drunk old Jew Churchill.'

Most of the boss's diatribes were directed against low- and middle-ranking Nazi Party officials, the so-called *Partei Kommune*, which he portrayed as selfish, corrupt and sexually depraved gangsters whose behaviour shamefully contrasted with 'the devotion to duty shown by our brave troops freezing to death in Russia'. He also addressed his comrades in the army, criticizing Germany's conduct in the war and denouncing all sorts of abuses.

One *GS1* broadcast in June 1941 complained of how Nazi Party officials were above the law, alleging that a Hitler Youth leader had been caught violating the 12-year-old daughter of a soldier, but no police action was taken against him. The next month, a detailed account was given on how *SS* men on the home front were being used to carry out 'race preservation'. What this meant was that German troops were being used to impregnate the widows of fallen soldiers to give them the children their dead husbands could not provide.

Another *GS1* programme attacked an *SS* man called Breuter who was in charge of children that had been evacuated from bombed German cities to Czechoslovakia. He was removed from his post after being found guilty of 67 charges of assaulting little girls. One 14-year-old he made pregnant died when a doctor performed an illegal abortion on her. Breuter had informed the girl's mother that she was a victim of scarlet fever. But despite this, *GS1* indignantly informed its listeners, Breuter had not been imprisoned but had instead been posted to Styria and was still in charge of child evacuees.

Then there was a report of an orgy held by a German admiral who took four or five sailors home with him, got them drunk and, to excite himself, had them sexually assault his mistress. They lubricated the action with butter, which was then rationed to ordinary people. The climax of the orgy was a detailed description of how the old admiral finally worked himself up into a state in which he, too, could have sex with the woman.

When Stafford Cripps, a puritanical member of Britain's war cabinet, discovered what Delmer was up to he said: 'If this is the sort of thing that is needed to win the war, why, I'd rather lose it.'

The station closed down in October 1943, its final broadcast involving a simulated raid on the radio's offices by gun-wielding Nazis. *GS1* was replaced by *Soldatensender Calais* ('Soldier Station Calais'), whose broadcasts were directed at German troops rather than the general public. It had music and sports reports, and even relayed speeches by Adolf Hitler and other Nazi officials. Its detailed reports of what was happening in Germany were gleaned from newspaper stories in occupied countries, the interrogation of prisoners of war, and aerial photography that showed which streets and even individual houses that been bombed in Allied raids.

The station warned of swindlers who were preying on soldiers who were being transferred to the Eastern Front and informed troops that, while they were away, their wives were sleeping with the foreign workers that had been brought into Germany.

After D-Day, when the Pas-de-Calais was overrun by the Allies, the station was renamed *Soldatensender West* (to preserve the illusion that it was operated by patriotic Germans). At the same time, another station called *Kurzwellensender Atlantik* was set up to broadcast to U-boat crews. Much of the material used in these broadcasts was reused in the newspaper *Nachrichten für die Truppe* ('News for the Troops'), which was dropped over Germany, Belgium and France each morning by the Special Leaflet Squadron of the US Eighth Air Force.

At the end of the war, Delmer advised his colleagues not to publicize the work they had been involved in, lest unrepentant Nazis claim that they had been defeated by underhand methods rather than on the battlefield, as they had after World War I. Delmer himself told all in his autobiography, published in the 1960s.

SS–UK

On 2 February 1943, Field Marshal Friedrich Paulus and the German Sixth Army surrendered at Stalingrad. It was Hitler's first major reverse and a turning point in the war. However, he still believed that Germany could win the conflict. To achieve that he needed the British and their American allies to change sides. With the Red Army now advancing westwards, Hitler surmised, they must have been aware of the danger to European civilization posed not by the Nazis but by the rampaging Communist forces of the Soviet Union.

What was needed was a band of Britons who would fight alongside the Germans on the Eastern Front. If such a force could be organized it would present a tremendous propaganda coup for the Nazis and persuade others to join forces in the battle against Communism. The elite *Waffen-SS* already boasted units of locals recruited in the occupied territories. Why not recruit a British *SS* unit alongside them?

The idea came from a shady character named John Amery, the son of Leo Amery, Secretary of State for India and Burma. In 1940, Leo Amery had brought down Neville Chamberlain's government, memorably telling the prime minister, in the words of Oliver Cromwell: 'You have sat here for too long for all the good you have been doing; depart, I say, and let us have done with you. In the name of God, go'. This intervention allowed Churchill to take over as Britain's war leader.

Leo's son John had fascist leanings. He had aligned himself with Franco during the Spanish Civil War and, based in France in the late 1930s, remained there after the German occupation. In September 1942, he went to Berlin where he suggested the formation of a British anti-Bolshevik legion. Hitler was impressed and allowed him to stay on in Germany, where he made a series of pro-German propaganda radio broadcasts, urging the British people to join the war against Communism.

Amery was a close friend of Jacques Doriot, leader of the *Légion des Volontaires Français*, which later became *33 SS-Waffen-Grenadier-Brigade der Charlemagne (französische Nr.1)*, a brigade of French volunteers fighting for the Germans and thought to have numbered as many as 11,000 men at its height.

Danish, Norwegian and Swedish volunteers had formed the *SS-Nordland* regiment, with Dutch and Flemish volunteers forming the *SS-Westland* regiment. The *Waffen-SS* also had a Finnish Volunteer Battalion. Volunteers to these formations came forward in such numbers that the *SS* had to open a new training camp solely for foreign recruits in Alsace-Lorraine. Together, they made up the bulk of *5 SS-Panzerdivision 'Wiking'*. Amery promised to recruit 1,500 Britons to fight Communism.

On 21 April 1943, he made a speech at an internment camp in the Parisian suburb of St Denis. Some 35 German-speaking internees had been gathered together in the camp theatre and handed a leaflet headed 'British National Presentation – Proclamation to all British Subjects Interned'. They were told they would be given 'a permanent well placed job in or priority in any employment they desired ... or the possibility to form the elite in the new British Army'. This pledge could be redeemed once a peace treaty between Britain and Germany was signed. Until then, they would have to fight alongside the *Waffen-SS*.

Amery told his audience that an RAF plane had flown from Britain three days earlier, carrying volunteers to join the British Legion of St George. If the internees signed up, they would be freed immediately, have a paid holiday and be given the right to unlimited numbers of letters and parcels to and from home. Hundreds were joining up from prisoner-of-war camps, he told them. Then he talked about the Soviet menace. Britain's only chance was to join the Third Reich in its war against Russia. Did they want to see the country they loved destroyed by Jews and Communists?

John Amery – would-be head of the British SS who was hanged for treason.

The speech was greeted by a stony silence. After all it was complete rubbish. There were no British planes flying over with men to join the Legion, nor were hundreds of British prisoners of war joining up in the camps.

Unfortunately, there was a man named Wilfred Brinkman in the audience who knew Amery from a time when the latter had been involved in a scam involving smuggling sterling cheques over the border into Spain. Brinkman remembered that, in that particular adventure, Amery had betrayed one of his accomplices to the police. What, Brinkman asked, would happen to any of Amery's recruits if they were captured? Amery had no answers.

As he left the camp, Amery was booed and jeered. The men forced to attend the meeting protested to the camp commandant. For a week, they were bombarded by anti-Communist propaganda. Amery then returned to the camp to speak to the men individually. Most did not believe a word he was saying. One did, however. Kenneth Berry was a gullible 17-year-old petty crook who had been a deckhand on SS *Cymbeline*, sunk by a German raider. When told by the camp commandant that Amery was the 'Foreign Secretary of England' he was suitably impressed and became the first recruit for the Legion of St George. Indeed, Berry was the only British subject that Amery managed to recruit during the entire war.

Amery then recruited 58-year-old Oswald Job, who had been born to German parents in Bromley, Kent. During World War I, he had been rejected for military service on medical grounds. He was working in Paris when the Germans invaded and arrested as an enemy alien. When Amery recruited Job, the Germans decided he was too valuable an asset to join the so-far imaginary Legion of St George. He was sent instead to England as a spy – where he was promptly arrested, tried and hanged.

The only other volunteer Amery signed up from St Denis was Maurice Tunmer, a French-born naturalized Englishman. As soon as Tunmer was released from the internment camp he made contact with the French Resistance. After crossing the border into Spain, he escaped to England and joined the Free French.

Undaunted, Amery and his German backers pressed on. British captives in prisoner-of-war camps were told about the Legion of St George and two special 'holiday camps' were set up where potential recruits would be given better food and more freedom. The man in charge of the new camps was Arnold Hillen-Ziegfeld, a German who had been interned on the Isle of Man during World War I. He needed a British NCO to run the first camp at Genshagen and recruited Battery Quartermaster Sergeant John Brown of the Royal Artillery. Captured during the retreat to Dunkirk on 29 May 1940, Brown had been a member of the British Union of Fascists before World War II, so it was assumed that he would be a useful collaborator.

As well as running a successful black-market operation, Brown was also a British spy, who pretended to cooperate with the Germans and sent sensitive information back to England in coded messages hidden in letters to his wife. Brown could hardly believe his luck when the opportunity came along to join what was now called the British Free Corps (it was renamed after Hitler had been persuaded that calling it the British Legion was not a good idea). Called to Berlin for an interview, Brown was able to roam the city freely, reporting back to London details of anti-aircraft installations and camouflaged defences, as well as the involvement of John Amery in what were surely treasonous activities.

When Germany attacked the Soviet Union in June 1941, Roy Courlander, a New Zealander who had been captured in Greece, claimed to be a White Russian émigré and volunteered to fight the Bolsheviks. Eventually he was taken to Berlin to meet John Amery, who explained the role of the Legion of St George to him. He volunteered to make propaganda broadcasts and was sent to Genshagen, thereby doubling his salary as a broadcaster and a recruiter for the Legion. Courlander told new inmates that Hitler had told them Britain would be defeated, Edward VIII would be returned to the throne and Oswald Mosley, leader of the British Union of Fascists (BUF), would become prime minister. The Duke of Windsor had been adopted as unofficial patron of the Legion.

Captured on Crete, Francis Maton, a Commando who had been a member of the BUF before the war, also made broadcasts before

Oswald Mosley – leader of the British Union of Fascists.

volunteering to fight the Bolsheviks. Arthur Chapple, a NAAFI manager, who maintained he was a lifelong socialist and anti-fascist, had been captured in France in 1940. While a prisoner, he met William Joyce, the Nazi propagandist 'Lord Haw-Haw', and volunteered to make propaganda broadcasts as his left-wing views ostensibly gave the station balance.

Thomas Cooper had an English father and a German mother. A member of the BUF, he had been on a trip to Germany when war was declared. Initially arrested as an enemy alien, it was quickly decided that he was an ethnic German, or *Volksdeutscher*. Foreigners could not join the German Army, but they could join the *Waffen-SS*. Using the name Böttcher, German for Cooper, he rose to become an *SS-Unterscharführer* and was wounded on the Eastern Front, so he turned up at Genshagen already in a German uniform. He bragged that, after Germany had won the war, he would be a Gauleiter, or provincial governor, in Nazi-occupied Britain.

Francis George McLardy was another member of the BUF. A sergeant in the Royal Medical Corps, he had been captured in Belgium in 1940. In the summer of 1943, he became ill. Convinced he would not survive another winter in the camp in Poland, he had written to the *Waffen-SS*, begging to join the fight against Bolshevism.

He arrived at Genshagen on 1 October 1943 with Edwin Barnard Martin, a private in the Canadian Army's Essex Scottish Regiment. He had been captured in the raid on Dieppe in August 1942 and collaborated with the Germans as a stoolpigeon, befriending new arrivals at the camp.

Alfred Minchin, a merchant seaman on an Arctic convoy, had been rescued by a German destroyer when his ship was sunk. He and five other prisoners were brought to Genshagen by former BUF member Frederick Lewis. There he met Cooper, who showed him recruitment posters for the new Legion and said that men were flocking to join.

When the camp was bombed, recruits were moved to a special compound at Luckenwalde, close to Berlin, where newly captured prisoners were interrogated while they were still disorientated and had not had time to get used to camp life. The chief interrogator there was a sergeant, or *feldwebel*, named Scharper. He was assisted by Private John Welch of the

Durham Light Infantry, who had been recruited after he was caught having sex with a German woman. This was a capital offence. He had a choice – execution or collaboration.

Trooper John Wilson of 3 Commando was captured during a raid to blow up a bridge in Calabria in August 1943. Hitler's notorious Commando Order, instructing that Commandos should be shot on sight, was in force, meaning that Wilson faced summary execution. Instead he found himself in a cell in Luckenwalde, where he was joined by Welch who pumped him for information. He was then given a stark choice: spend the rest of the war in solitary confinement or join the Legion, which he was told was now 30,000 strong. He joined.

Brown objected to underhanded recruitment methods like these, convincing Cooper that men recruited by trickery would be little use on the battlefield. He took to subtly persuading potential recruits it was not in their interests to join; those who did not display the requisite levels of pro-German or pro-Nazi sympathies were sent to an isolation camp in Mecklenberg. By November 1943, the now-renamed British Free Corps numbered just 22 men.

SS-Hauptsturmführer Hans Werner Roepke was appointed the Corps' commanding officer. He spoke good English, having spent a year as an exchange student in the US, though this hardly equipped him to understand the British and their ways. The SS had wanted a British CO. Courlander volunteered, but like Hitler he was only a lance-corporal and therefore not considered officer material.

At a meeting with Roepke, Cooper, Courlander, McLardy, Martin, Minchin and Wilson – known among the legionnaires as the 'Big Six' – agreed that, even as SS men, they would not swear allegiance to Adolf Hitler as they had already sworn an oath to the British Crown. Nor would they have their blood group tattooed on their armpit like other SS men. If captured, this would be clear proof of treachery.

Eight hundred uniforms with BFC insignia were ordered from the SS clothing stores. But with some men involved in broadcast propaganda and others still manning the holiday camp at Genshagen, the main body of the BFC numbered just nine. They were sent to a Nordic Study Centre in the small town of Hildesheim where, out of reach of German officers, they drank beer and chased local girls. When the refuseniks in the Mecklenberg isolation camp heard what they were missing, some rapidly rethought their loyalties and rejoined the unit.

The aim now was to get the BFC up to its fighting strength of 30, so Cooper, Minchin, Berry and others set out on a recruitment drive. They found two volunteers at a seamen's internment camp, or Milag, near Bremen. Herbert George Rowlands had fought in the International Brigade during the Spanish Civil War, but he was in solitary confinement and took little persuading. And Ronald David Barker had been an Australian cabin boy on the MV *British Advocate* when it was captured by the *Admiral von Scheer* in the Indian Ocean in 1941. In the camp, he had become friendly with a young woman in the censorship office and was told that they would both be sent to concentrations camps unless he joined.

At the camp, Berry met some former shipmates from the *Cymbeline* who told him that the prospects for Germany were not quite as rosy as Nazi propaganda portrayed them. He then wrote a letter to the senior British officer at the Milag, saying that he had made a mistake.

Former BUF member and small-time criminal Eric Pleasants was arrested several times on Jersey in 1941 and 1942, along with his partner in crime, safecracker Eddie Chapman. While Chapman would go on to find a degree of fame – or infamy – as agent Zigzag, a German spy who became a British double agent, Pleasants' wartime career was not so colourful. Deported from Jersey to France, Pleasants was moved from internment camp to internment camp, where he constantly managed to fall foul of the authorities and was branded a troublemaker. He ended up at the seamen's Milag just when the BFC arrived on its mission to find new members. He happily joined up, not, so he later claimed, to fight for the Nazis but to give himself the opportunity to be sent to the Eastern Front, where he could defect to the Soviets and be repatriated to Britain. On his only job for the SS – a mission to Denmark – he got drunk before he reached the border.

Members of the British Free Corps – Kenneth Berry and Alfred Minchin.

Another, more successful, recruit was Private Thomas Freeman of 7 Commando – although not for the reasons John Amery would have liked. As a BFC member, Freeman took it upon himself to sabotage the unit from within. Edwin Barnard Martin was one of his first 'victims', with Freeman doing such a good job undermining his morale that he resigned from the Corps and asked to be transferred to the Mecklenberg isolation camp. Freeman was a plausible character and the BFC's leaders did not suspect he was up to anything untoward. In fact, he was given a role trying to recruit new members and he used his position to only sign up men he believed would help him damage the unit. Among these were Corporal Albert Stokes of the Australian Army and Sergeant Theo Ellsmore, a Belgian national pretending to be a South African. Equally unimpressed with the BFC were James Conen, a London taxi driver, and William Celliers, a policeman from Namibia, both of whom were sent to join the organization after serving in Russia with an anti-aircraft detachment of the *Leibstandarte Adolf Hitler*.

A sign of the unit's true commitment to the Nazi cause came when its members were presented with their uniforms in time for a parade celebrating Hitler's birthday. The men refused to wear them. One particular grievance was that the left sleeve bore a German eagle carrying a swastika above the Union flag. When a recruit said it looked as though the eagle was defecating on the British flag, the men's complaint had to be taken up with Himmler himself, who authorized the Union flag being moved to the right arm.

Soon, and struggling to attract new members, the BFC's recruiters were forced to lower their standards. Private Hugh Cowie of the Gordon Highlanders had been working as a tractor driver in Poland when he seized the opportunity to flee from his prisoner-of-war detail and make a dash for the Russian lines. He was caught a few miles short of his objective and joined the BFC to escape punishment. Frederick Croft of the Royal Artillery had spent long terms in solitary confinement for numerous escape attempts. Private Edward Jackson of the King's Own Royal Regiment was picked up by the Gestapo after he disappeared from a working party to be with his girlfriend, while Charlie Munns of the Durham Light Infantry would otherwise have faced a firing squad after getting his girlfriend pregnant.

Perhaps the pick of the bunch was Lieutenant William Shearer of the Seaforth Highlanders, the only officer to join the BFC. He had been recruited from a mental hospital, but he refused to come out of his room and had to be repatriated on medical grounds.

News of the D-Day landings lowered morale even further. Roy Courlander and Francis Maton inveigled their way out of the BFC to join *SS-Standarte Kurt Eggers*, the war correspondents' unit covering the Western Front. But this was just a smokescreen to mask their real intentions. After taking a train from Berlin to Brussels, they were put up in a series of safe houses until the Allies arrived to liberate Belgium. They became the first BFC men to make it home. Other escape attempts failed.

They were replaced by Private Harry Nightingale of the Royal Artillery and William Alexander of the Highland Light Infantry. Both had been forced to join the BFC to escape punish for sexual liaisons with German girls. Despite still being under strength, the BFC was sent to the *Waffen-SS* Pioneer school in Dresden for military training.

As it was now clear that Germany was going to lose the war, Thomas Cooper and John Wilson agreed to go to the *SS-Hauptamt*, or Main Office, in Berlin and ask to be returned to an ordinary prisoner-of-war camp. But Wilson really wanted to go to Berlin to see his girlfriend, and when Cooper turned up alone at the *SS-Hauptamt* he was arrested and charged with attempting to sabotage the BFC. As a punishment, he was sent to work as a military policeman in a *Leibstandarte Adolf Hitler* depot. Wilson, meanwhile, replaced Thomas Freeman as senior NCO. On recruiting trips, he called himself RSM Montgomery MM, variously claiming to be Field Marshal Bernard Montgomery's brother, son or nephew.

Despite Germany's imminent collapse in the war, odd waifs and strays continued to volunteer for the BFC. One of them was William Miller of the Royal Artillery, who had been captured at Tobruk. He joined to avoid a four-month sentence in a German military prison. By January 1945, the BFC's numbers had swelled to 27. Ronald Barker, an Australian prisoner of war who only signed up with the unit as he thought it would offer him better access to alcohol and women, returned drunk to his barracks one night and beat up the guard on duty. This did nothing to improve the BFC's *esprit de corps*. Private Edward Jackson of the King's Own Royal Regiment signed up for the BFC because the Gestapo caught him skiving off his prisoner-of-war work detail to visit his girlfriend in Dresden.

Frank Axon of the Royal Army Service Corps had been captured in Greece in 1941. In captivity he had been employed as an agricultural worker and was accused of slapping a cow and making it calve early. Found guilty of cruelty to a farm animal, he was told to join the BFC or face punishment.

Then there were the six Maoris who tried to join up, largely because they wanted to fight New Zealand's white government. This would have pushed the strength of the BFC over its threshold of 30 to officially make it a platoon. Unfortunately, it had to be explained delicately to the antipodean warriors that the *SS* was a 'whites only' organization.

Even though the BFC had still not reached its required platoon strength, the German top brass decided it was time for it to go into action. This focused some of the recruits' minds – and they immediately asked to be transferred to the isolation camp or to the *SS-Standarte Kurt Eggers*. John Wilson, who was suffering from a dose of gonorrhoea, landed a cushy liaison role. Of the ten remaining men, two were left behind on the grounds that they were useless, while Minchin was in hospital with scabies. After a four-day course on using the *Panzerfaust* – a hand-held recoilless anti-tank gun – Ronald Barker lost his enthusiasm for fighting for Germany, smoked some aspirin in order to make himself ill and took to his sickbed.

On their way to the Eastern Front, the remaining men cut the BFC insignia off their uniforms. At Stettin, they presented themselves at the headquarters of the *(Germanisches) SS-Panzer-Korps*, which still contained the remnants of the *Nordland* division and the Dutch *Niederland* brigade. Even so, the German commanders were a little taken aback to be presented with British reinforcements. While there they suffered another casualty. Frederick Croft, who had volunteered for the *Totenkopf*, or Death's Head unit, came down with gonorrhoea and was sent to the military hospital in

Neubrandenburg. His girlfriend said she had caught it from Wilson, who had raped her.

On 22 March 1945, the last BFC stragglers were sent to join an armoured reconnaissance battalion, where they were greeted by the much-decorated *Sturmbannführer* Rudolf Saalback, who had been with the SS since 1932. They were put under the command of *Obersturmführer* Hans-Gösta Pehrson, a Swede, and issued an amphibious jeep and an armoured personnel carrier. The division was being rested in preparation for the next Soviet offensive, but there was a shortage of food and ammunition, so the men bartered some cigarettes for bullets to go and shoot deer in the forest.

The South African, Douglas Cecil Mardon, now in command, was keen to get on with the fighting, though the others were more reticent. He called them 'yellow bastards'. Then Thomas Cooper turned up. He persuaded corps commander *SS-Obergruppenführer* Felix Steiner that, given their composition and competence, the BFC would be useless in a combat role. Steiner gave them a rousing speech about how Britain and Germany would one day unite and conquer the world, then decided to use them as truck drivers.

With not a shot fired in anger, the BFC was pulled out of the line. Next a tall, blond-haired Englishman wearing the black uniform of an SS tank regiment arrived. He introduced himself as *Hauptsturmführer* Douglas Berneville-Claye and said he had come to lead them into battle.

Born plain Douglas Claye, the unit's new CO was a conman. As well as adopting a double-barrelled surname, he sometimes also styled himself as Lord Charlesworth. Before he was captured by the Germans, Claye had volunteered to serve with the SAS. But he was generally considered so useless that his fellow soldiers refused to go on operations with him.

Addressing his BFC men, Claye told them he had been authorized by the British government to fight the Russians. They did not have to worry that they would be in trouble with the British authorities as Britain would be at war with the Soviet Union in a few days, he claimed.

Thomas Cooper called his bluff. 'You've come to drop them back in the shit after I have just got them out of it?' he said.

The game was up. Seconding a driver, Claye turned around and headed for the American lines, changing back into an SAS uniform on the way. The day before Hitler committed suicide, Steiner and his men pulled out too. Cooper was now the senior NCO in the transport company, so the BFC led the evacuation westwards. They ditched their uniforms before they reached Allied lines. No one was fooled.

MI5 had been compiling a list of the traitors. John Amery and Thomas Cooper would face prosecution for treason, alongside William Joyce and another broadcaster named Walter Purdy. Amery and Joyce were sentenced to death and hanged. Cooper and Purdy were also sentenced to death, but reprieved. Cooper served seven years, Purdy eight.

Those still in uniform were given shorter sentences. It was not considered worthwhile recalling those who had already been demobbed, so MI5 invited them in and told them not to do it again.

THE DUQUESNE SPY RING

While the British managed to arrest or turn German spies during the war, the Americans managed to roll up a massive ring of Nazi spies on US soil before they had even fired a shot in anger. The spies were largely German immigrants who had naturalized and worked in industry and the docks, which were prime targets for sabotage. They also reported on engineering developments and shipping bound for Britain while German U-boats preyed on merchantmen in the Battle of the Atlantic.

The ring was run by Frederick 'Fritz' Jourbert Duquesne. A South African Boer, he had fought in the Second Anglo-Boer War of 1899–1902. Captured during a daring attempt to assassinate the British chief of staff Lord Kitchener, he was sent to the penal colony on Bermuda, but he escaped to the US in 1902, where he became a journalist on the *New York Herald*. He naturalized in 1913.

During World War I, he went to Brazil where he sabotaged British ships. It is said that he eventually succeeded in killing Kitchener, joining him on HMS *Hampshire* disguised as a Russian duke, then signalling to a German U-boat that torpedoed the cruiser. He escaped on a life raft, was picked up by the submarine and was awarded the Iron Cross and the rank of colonel.

When he was arrested for insurance fraud in 1917, he had in his possession a large file of news clippings concerning bomb explosions on ships, as well as a letter from the German Assistant Vice Consul at Managua, Nicaragua, saying that, 'Captain Duquesne' was 'one who has rendered considerable service to the German cause'. The British demanded his extradition, but he escaped and fled to Mexico. Returning to the US under a false name, he became an intelligence officer for an American pro-Nazi organization called the Order of '76, which claimed to have 100,000 members.

Head of the *Abwehr* Admiral Wihelm Canaris sent Colonel Nikolas Ritter to contact Duquesne in New York in 1937 to ask him to set up a spy ring. Then, in February 1940, Ritter sent William Sebold to join it with instructions to set up a short-wave station to transmit information back to Germany.

Sebold had served in the German army in World War I, but emigrated to America in 1922 and naturalized in 1936. Returning to Germany to visit his mother in 1939, Sebold was approached by Ritter, who coerced him into becoming a spy. After seven weeks' training in Hamburg, he was sent back to the US to contact Duquesne. But even before he left Germany, Sebold contacted the US Consul General and offered to become a double agent.

Back in the States, he provided information on the Duquesne Spy Ring direct to the FBI. There was one member among them that the Americans were particularly interested in – an attractive, bleach-blonde woman named Lilly Stein. Born into a wealthy Jewish family in Austria, she was a wild child who became estranged from her family and made a living as an artists' life model. She travelled with a sugar daddy called Heinrich Sorau, whose real name was Captain Hermann Sandel. Codenamed Uncle Hugo, he was the head of the spy school in Hamburg that had trained William Sebold.

As war approached, it was thought that an attractive young woman could be of use in the *Abwehr*. After training, Sandel furnished her with a German passport that classified her as 'Jewish first-degree mixture', a so-called *Mischling*, one of the 'half-Jews' who were initially spared the worst of the anti-Semitic persecution. A US visa was provided by Ogden Hammond Jr, the 27-year-old US vice-consul in Vienna.

In October 1939, she arrived in New York and checked into the fashionable Windsor Hotel. From there, she sent a letter to the lynchpin of

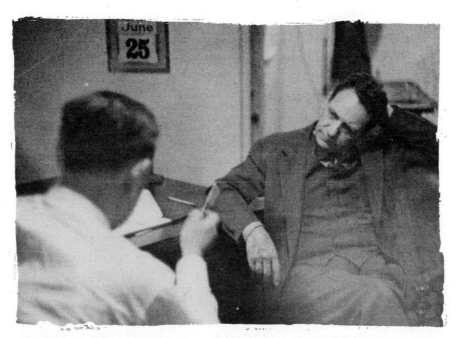

William Sebold (left) talks to Frederick Duquesne.

the Duquesne Spy Ring, Else Weustenfeld, a German-born naturalized US citizen who lived with Hans W. Ritter, the brother of Nikolaus Ritter.

The two women met at the Windsor Hotel. Lilly had microfilm carrying instructions for Duquesne as well as money for him. She then found an apartment on West Eighty-First Street, where she handed over the microphotograph and the money. The apartment would be used as a return address by other agents in mailing information to Germany.

Stein set up an exclusive shop that attracted the wives of wealthy industrialists and financiers. She also frequented the best hotels, nightclubs and theatres in search of influential men, extracting information via pillow talk or through blackmail. It was easy work. One FBI agent who had her under surveillance described her as a 'well-built, good-looking nymphomaniac with a sense of humour'. The prudish FBI chief J. Edgar Hoover dismissed her as a 'Viennese prostitute'.

Thanks to Sebold, the FBI were soon on to her. She was one of the agents Sebold was to deliver microphotographic equipment to when he returned to the States. He phoned and took a cab to her apartment. The door was answered by a good-looking 24-year-old woman with a seductive manner.

A few days later, they met in a restaurant where she told him she was in the midst of a dalliance with the American diplomat Ogden Hammond Jr, who had provided her visa and had now been recalled from Austria. He told her that there was 'no chance of America getting into the war'.

Not all the intelligence she supplied was duff. On 3 September 1940, at the height of the Battle of Britain, she informed Sebold that British factories were producing 1,000 planes a month. The source of this information was Captain Hubert Martineau, a British cricketer and military officer she was consorting with. This was sensitive information on Britain's war effort. Sebold did not transmit it back to Germany.

As the information Stein was getting out of Hammond was next to useless, Sebold was told to dump her. Soon after, Hammond was called in by Assistant Secretary of State Adolf Berle who told him he knew all about his affair with Lilly Stein. Hammond was asked to resign. He refused, swearing that, 'at no time did I live with … or have intimate relations with' Lilly Stein. He took out an injunction against the State Department, but it was circulated in the press that he had 'disloyal dealings' with an unnamed 'female agent of a foreign power'. He sued, but lost his case and was refused permission to appeal to the Supreme Court.

Lilly was still in touch with Else Weustenfeld. Neither of them trusted Sebold, suspecting that he was embezzling money. Stein even thought he might be a double agent, but Weustenfeld said he wasn't brave enough to do that.

With Sebold's credibility dented, the FBI decided to round up the Duquesne Spy Ring. On 27 June 1941, some 250 special agents pounced. That evening, Stein was entertaining a gentleman caller – a person of 'considerable importance', the FBI noted.

Raymond Newkirk, who was assigned to interrogate her, said: 'Lilly thought it a big joke. She knew she was going to jail but was satisfied that she had made enough money to make it worthwhile. She figured she had taken the Germans for a ride because she was always hollering for money for information she knew wasn't worth a damn.'

J. Edgar Hoover described the investigation as 'the greatest of its kind in the nation's history' and the largest since the enactment of the 1917 Espionage Act. He told a press conference that 'artists' model' Lilly Stein was the unnamed agent mentioned in press accounts of the Ogden Hammond Jr case.

Pleading guilty, Stein was sentenced to ten years for espionage with another two years for failing to register under the 1938 Foreign Agents Registration Act. She was eventually deported back to Austria and became one of the few Austrian Jews to survive the Holocaust.

Duquesne was charged with espionage. On one occasion he provided Sebold with photographs and specifications of a new type of bomb being produced in the United States. He claimed that he secured the material by secretly entering the DuPont plant in Wilmington, Delaware. Duquesne also explained how fires could be started in industrial plants. Much of the information Duquesne obtained was the result of his correspondence with industrial concerns. Representing himself as a student, he requested data concerning their products and manufacturing conditions.

Not only were the ring's members collecting sensitive information and passing it to the Germans, they were preparing acts of sabotage. One of the spies was preparing a bomb of his own and even delivered dynamite and detonation caps to Sebold.

Duquesne was brought to trial and was convicted. He was sentenced to 18 years for espionage, plus a two-year concurrent sentence and payment of a $2,000 fine for violation of the Registration Act. His live-in girlfriend Evelyn Clayton Lewis had helped Duquesne prepare material for transmittal abroad. She pleaded guilty and was sentenced to serve one year and one day in prison for violation of the Registration Act.

Else Weustenfeld was sentenced to five years' imprisonment on a charge of espionage and two concurrent years on a charge of registration violations. Alfred E. Brokhoff, a mechanic for the United States Lines shipping company in New York City, got five years for helping Paul Fehse secure information about the sailing dates and cargoes of ships heading for England, and for assisting Fehse in transmitting the information to Germany. Fehse was caught while attempting to flee the country and was sentenced to 15 years, plus one year and one day in prison for violation of the Registration Act.

Conradin Otto Dodd, chief steward aboard the SS *Siboney* of the American Export Lines shipping company, got ten years for carrying information from Nazi agents in the United States to contacts in neutral ports abroad for transmittal to Germany, plus a two-year concurrent sentence and a fine of $1,000 for violation of the Registration Act.

Rene Emanuel Mezenen, a Frenchman who claimed US citizenship through the naturalization of his father, also acted as a courier. The German Intelligence Service in Lisbon, Portugal, had recruited Mezenen to carry information on his regular trips on the transatlantic clipper, a flying boat service between the United States and Portugal. In the course of flights across the Atlantic, Mezenen also observed the convoys sailing to Britain and reported the sightings. He got eight years with two concurrent years for registration violations.

Another courier was Oscar Richard Stabler, who worked as a barber aboard transoceanic ships. In December 1940, British authorities in Bermuda found a map of Gibraltar in his possession. He was detained for a short period before being released. Then he was picked up by the FBI for transmitting information between German agents in the United States and contacts abroad. He was sentenced to five years for espionage with a two-year concurrent term under the Registration Act.

Hartwig Richard Kleiss got five years for providing blueprints of the SS *America*, which showed the locations of newly installed gun emplacements. He included information about how guns would be brought into position for firing. Kleiss also obtained details on the construction and performance of new speedboats being developed by the United States Navy, which he gave to Sebold for transmission to Germany.

Erwin Wilhelm Sielger, the chief butcher on the SS *America*, a cruise liner later used as a troop ship, got ten years for providing the money to buy a bomb sight. He also obtained information about the movement of ships and military defence preparations for the Panama Canal. Also on board, until the US Navy converted the ship into USS *West Point*, was Franz Joseph

The convicted members of the Duquesne Spy Ring.

Stigler. He sought to recruit amateur radio operators in the United States as channels of communication to German receiving stations. He also observed and reported on defence preparations in the Canal Zone, and got 16 years on espionage charges with two concurrent years for registration violations.

Herman W. Lang got 18 years. He had been employed by a company manufacturing highly confidential materials essential to the national defence of the United States. During a visit to Germany in 1938, Lang conferred with German military authorities and reconstructed plans of the confidential materials from memory.

Carl Reuper was an inspector for the Westinghouse Electric Company in Newark, New Jersey. He obtained photographs for Germany relating to national defence materials and construction, and arranged for radio contact with Germany through Sebold and others. He got 16 years for espionage plus two years concurrent under the Registration Act. Another 16 years was handed to Everett Minster Roeder, a draughtsman and designer of confidential materials for the US Army and Navy. Born American, he gave classified information to the Germans for money.

Paul Alfred W. Scholz, who had not taken US citizenship, had arranged for the construction of a radio set to transmit the information provided by others back to Germany. He got 16 years for espionage plus a concurrent sentence of two years under the Registration Act. One of those who helped build the radio set was Axel Wheeler-Hill. He got 15 years plus two concurrent years under the Registration Act. Felix Jahnke, who used the radio set to transmit coded messages from his apartment in the Bronx, which were then intercepted by the FBI, got 20 months and a $1,000 fine.

Erich Strunck, a seaman with United States Lines, had planned to steal the diplomatic bag of a British officer travelling aboard his ship and push the officer overboard until Sebold convinced him that it would be too risky. Nevertheless, he got ten years for espionage plus a two-year concurrent term under the Registration Act.

Leo Waalen gathered information about ships sailing for England. He also obtained a confidential booklet issued by the FBI that contained precautions to be taken by industrial plants to safeguard national defence materials from sabotage. Waalen also secured government contracts listing specifications for materials and equipment, as well as detailed sea charts of the United States' Atlantic coastline. He got 12 years, plus a concurrent two-year term for violation of the Registration Act.

George Gottlob Schuh sent information directly to the Gestapo in Hamburg. He reported that Winston Churchill had arrived in the United States on the HMS *George V* and furnished information to Germany concerning the movement of ships carrying materials and supplies to Britain. He got just 18 months, plus a $1,000 fine.

Others got short sentences – 18 months, two years – for obtaining books on magnesium and aluminium alloys and writing to people in Europe. But then America was not, yet, at war. There were, in all, 33 conspirators in the Duquesne Spy Ring.

When they were picked up, the FBI had an airtight case. Nineteen quickly pleaded guilty. The remaining 14 were brought to trial in Brooklyn on 3 September 1941. They were all found guilty by a jury on 13 December 1941 – after the attack on Pearl Harbor and Germany had declared war on the United States. On 2 January 1942, they were sentenced to a total of more than 300 years in prison. As a result, America entered the war confident that there was no major German espionage network operating within its borders.

But while the FBI boss called the bureau's swoop on Duquesne's ring the greatest spy roundup in history, in a 1942 memo to his superiors Canaris wrote that Duquesne had 'delivered valuable reports and important technical material in the original, including U.S. gas masks, radio-controlled apparatus, leakproof fuel tanks, television instruments, small bombs for airplanes versus airplanes, air separator, and propeller-driving mechanisms. Items delivered were labelled "valuable", and several "good" and "very good"'.

THE BOMBING OF COVENTRY

On the night of 14 November 1940, the Luftwaffe made a devastating bombing raid on the city of Coventry. In the previous months there had been a number of smaller raids, killing 176 people and injuring 680. But, on that night, the Germans sent 515 bombers with the intention of destroying Coventry's vital factories and industrial infrastructure.

The city was located by German radio beams. Pathfinder planes were then sent and dropped incendiary bombs to mark the target. Then, heavy bombers dropped high explosive bombs. These were designed to shatter roofs, so that incendiaries carried by further waves would have a better chance of setting the buildings on fire. They also cratered the roads and damaged the water mains, hampering the fire brigades sent to extinguish the blazes.

The medieval Coventry Cathedral was hit at around 8 pm. Firefighters managed to extinguish the first blaze, but further attacks created a fire storm. The raid reached its climax at around midnight, but continued until the all-clear was sounded at around 6.15 the following morning.

The Daimler factory, the Humber Hillman factory, and the Alfred Herbert Ltd machine tool works were destroyed, along with nine aircraft factories and two naval ordnance stores. However, the effects on war production were only temporary. Much essential war production had already been moved to 'shadow factories' on the city's outskirts. Many of the damaged factories were quickly repaired and returned to full production within a few months.

More than 4,300 homes were destroyed and two-thirds of the city's buildings were damaged. An estimated 568 people were killed in the raid and 1,256 injured. This was comparatively light as, after the earlier bombing raid, many people moved out of the city at night to sleep in the surrounding towns and villages, or took to air raid shelters.

The destruction was such that Nazi Propaganda Minister Joseph Goebbels coined the term 'coventriet' ('coventried') and threatened to do the same to other British cities. In response, the British began the area bombing of German cities, resulting in far worse devastation.

On the night of the attack Coventry was defended by just two dozen 3.7 inch heavy anti-aircraft guns and 12 lighter 40 mm Bofors quick-firing guns. These brought down just one German plane. Radar was in its infancy and the British failed to disrupt the German radio location beams that night.

It has been alleged that Churchill knew that Coventry would be targeted from the Ultra decrypts emanating from Bletchley Park but did not warn the city or increase its defences in case the Germans realized that the British had broken the Enigma code. The story was first told by Group Captain F.W. Winterbottom, who had been in charge of distributing Ultra intelligence, in his book *The Ultra Secret* published in 1974. It was the first book to reveal that the British had broken the German codes. Winterbottom said that the name Coventry appeared in an Ultra decrypt at 3 pm on 14 November and he immediately telephoned one of Churchill's private secretaries in Downing Street.

The following year, British journalist Anthony Cave Brown published *Bodyguard of Lies*, which said that Churchill received the Ultra decrypt two days before the raid. It identified three proposed targets. One was codenamed 'All One Price' – a slogan used by the budget department store Woolworths, hence Wolverhampton. The second was 'umbrella' – a reference to Neville Chamberlain, who was never seen without an umbrella and was mayor of Birmingham before he became prime minister. The third was 'Corn', which turned out to be Coventry.

Then, in 1977's *A Man Called Intrepid*, the biography of Sir William Stephenson, the head of British intelligence in the United States during

Winston Churchill at Coventry after the bombing.

World War II, the Canadian author William Stevenson said that Stephenson had given the Ultra decrypt to Churchill personally and advised him not to evacuate the city. Ultra was too valuable a source of intelligence to risk being compromised. Coventry was to be left to the mercy of the Luftwaffe, rather than reveal that the secret German codes had been broken.

Stephenson also played a part in the creation of James Bond. Although the British were not supposed to be spying in the United States, Stephenson, a Canadian, set up the British Security Coordination Office in the Rockefeller Center, which ran all British intelligence in the Western hemisphere.

A decorated fighter pilot in World War I and a European lightweight amateur boxing champion, Stephenson had become a millionaire by the time he was 30, having invented a way to transmit photographs by radio.

Ian Fleming, a British intelligence officer at this time, was fascinated by Stephenson's operation in New York and his secret Station M in Canada, which produced technical gadgets and forged documents.

In August 1941, Ian Fleming was in New York while Stephenson was preparing a secret mission. The Japanese consulate was on the floor below Stephenson's office in the Rockefeller Center. A cipher clerk there was sending coded messages back to Tokyo by short-wave radio, and Stephenson found out about this and began to study his movements, noting when he came and left the building. Stephenson had duplicate keys to the consulate made and, one night at 3 am, he and Fleming broke in to the office, microfilmed the code books and returned them to the safe they had removed them from. In *Casino Royale*, James Bond reveals that he had earned his double-0 number after killing a cipher expert in the Rockefeller Center.

According to Fleming, Stephenson also mixed the largest dry martinis in America and served them in quart glasses. He was undoubtedly an influence. In a letter to the *Sunday Times* in 1962, Fleming said, 'James Bond is a highly romanticized version of a true spy. The real thing is … William Stephenson.'

Furthermore, Stephenson had another plan to get his hands on $3 million in gold belonging to the Vichy government held on the Caribbean island of Martinique, which may have helped inspire *Goldfinger*. The operation never came to fruition.

Before the bombing of Coventry, the British Air Ministry was aware that the Luftwaffe was planning a new strategy. On 11 November, the Air Ministry received a decoded German message referring to a raid with the codename 'Moonlight Sonata'. This was the message in which the word 'Corn' first appeared. Dr R.V. Jones, one of the Air Ministry scientists working on the problem of the German bombers, felt that 'Corn' referred not to a target but to the appearance of radar screens when the signal was being jammed.

The 'Moonlight Sonata' codename for the operation indicated that the raid would take place on a night when there was a full moon. That meant that it would take place between 15 and 20 November. 'Sonata' indicated that the raid would be in three parts and the Air Ministry considered that this meant that the first part would be the fire-raisers and the other two parts would be normal bombing raids. No one at the Air Ministry felt that 'Sonata' referred to three quite separate targets on three separate nights.

Another decrypt mentioned four potential targets. They were all thought to be in the south of England, particularly London. This seemed to be confirmed by a captured German map that had four target areas marked on it. Intelligence gathered from a prisoner of war that Coventry and other targets in the Midlands were objectives for a future raid were not connected by the Ministry with the 'Moonlight Sonata' decrypt.

In the early hours of 12 November, Dr Jones received a decrypt of another German message which indicated that there was to be a raid against Coventry, Wolverhampton and Birmingham. But, again, there was nothing in the message to connect it with 'Moonlight Sonata'. Nor was the connection made. The Air Ministry was still expecting a raid on London.

Dr Jones, who published *Most Secret War* in 1979, got the Ultra decrypts at the same time as Winterbottom and says he never saw the message Winterbottom referred to. When he went home that night he was still wondering where the attack was going to come.

Churchill certainly thought that the raid was going to be on London. As he was preparing to leave Downing Street for his country home at Enstone in Oxfordshire he was handed a report from the Air Ministry which he took with him to read in the car. He did not get very far. After reading the document he ordered his driver to turn around and go back to Downing Street, explaining to his aide that the Air Ministry expected a major German raid on the capital that night. After sending his staff away to a shelter, accompanied by his chief military assistant General Sir Hastings Ismay, Churchill went to the Air Ministry roof and waited for the bombers that never came.

CAMOUFLAGING THE SUEZ CANAL

While the *Afrika Korps* under Ewin Rommel was in North Africa from March 1941 to May 1943, it had two main objectives. One was to block the Suez Canal to cut Britain off from its empire in India, Australasia and the Far East. The second was to push on and join up with the army coming through Russia and the Caucasus to take the oil fields of the Middle East. Petrol was a vital commodity in mechanized warfare, a commodity Germany was perilously short of.

While the British Eighth Army managed to hold the *Afrika Korps* back, the Germans were often within bombing range of the canal. Its defence fell to a stage magician named Jasper Maskelyne. In one of the greatest feats of deception of the war, he made the Suez Canal and Alexandria, a vital port for supplies, simply disappear.

Maskelyne came from a family of magicians. He was adept at sleight of hand, card and rope tricks, and 'mind-reading'. In 1936, he published *Maskelyne's Book of Magic* describing his stage tricks. The following year, he performed his famous trick – appearing to swallow razor blades and retrieve them tied along a thread – for Pathé.

When war broke out, he joined the Royal Engineers. After an unsuccessful spell at the Camouflage Development and Training Centre at Farnham he was recruited by MI9, the intelligence section concerned with prisoners of war, which sent him to Cairo to produce gadgets that could be used to help prisoners escape and evade recapture.

The British needed to protect the harbour at Alexandria and the Royal

Navy ships moored there from Axis bombing. Hiding it by day would be difficult, given its sheer size, but night-time bombing runs when the defences were hampered by darkness would be different. Despite the harbour's size, Maskelyne constructed a decoy of it using mud, cardboard and canvas at Maryut Bay several miles away, complete with fake docks and ships. When supply ships arrived at Alexandria, the lights there would be switched off and the ones at Maryut turned on to confuse Nazi pilots.

To make the Suez Canal invisible to enemy bombers, his idea of using mirrors was rejected. Instead, Maskelyne came up with the unorthodox solution of constructing 21 'dazzle lights' along the length of the canal. These powerful searchlights, containing 24 different spinning beams, projected a swirling, cartwheeling confusion of light up to 14.5 km (9 miles) into the sky, creating what Maskelyne called 'Whirling Spray'. The barrage of light was designed to confuse and blind the enemy bombers.

One dazzle light was constructed, but in the event regular search lights proved effective enough in disorientating enemy pilots. The Suez Canal is a narrow strip of water and it makes for a difficult target for high-level bombers at night. It was not hit during the war.

In the build-up to the crucial Battle of El Alamein, it was vital that Rommel did not know what the British were planning. The task of fooling the Germans fell to the Middle East Command Camouflage Directorate, commanded by Major Geoffrey Barkas, an Oscar-winning film director. The Surrealist Roland Penrose tutored the band of painters, cartoonists and sculptors at the directorate, while his lover Lee Miller, posing nude in camouflage cream and netting, served as inspiration. Maskelyne worked with them briefly, tasked with concocting some experimental concepts.

For El Alamein, he came up with the idea of the 'sunshield'. This was a light canvas construction put on top of a tank to make it look like a truck. Trucks were then fitted with wooden constructions to make them look like tanks.

The tanks disguised as trucks moved north to where the main attack was going to come, while the trucks disguised as tanks moved south. A dummy pipeline was laid using petrol cans. Only a short section had to be

Jasper Maskelyne – the conjurer who used magic to aid the war effort.

A 'sunshield tank' made to look like a truck to fool enemy air reconnaissance before El Alamein.

visible from the air each day. This was moved forward every night, making it appear that the previous section had been buried. Progress was timed so that it looked as if the pipeline would be completed in November 1942, although the attack would actually come in October.

Similarly, dummy field guns were made. The camouflage was allowed to slip so that the German reconnaissance planes would see they were dummies. Then they would be replaced with real guns. The effect was that the Germans split their forces. As a result, the British won the battle. As Churchill said: 'Before Alamein we never had a victory. After Alamein we never had a defeat.' And it had been achieved, partially at least, by sleight of hand.

OPERATION MINCEMEAT

As the Allied campaign in North Africa drew to a successful conclusion in 1942, the Western Allies had to figure out what to do next. As it was clear that no landings in northwest France could be mounted until 1944, British Prime Minister Winston Churchill suggested that they attack the 'soft underbelly of Europe'. This meant either invading Italy, or the Balkans through Greece.

When Churchill and US President Franklin D. Roosevelt met at the Casablanca Conference in January 1943, they decided that the next target should be Sicily. That would give the Allies control of the Mediterranean and be a stepping stone to mainland Italy. The problem was that it was too damn obvious. 'Everyone but a bloody fool would know that it's Sicily,' said Churchill.

Everyone but that bloody fool Hitler. He particularly feared an invasion of the Balkans as it would rob him of the raw materials needed for the German war effort – copper, bauxite, chrome and oil. To play into his fears, the fictitious Twelfth Army was established with its headquarters in Cairo. It's 12 non-existent divisions went on manoeuvres in Syria, deploying dummy armoured vehicles and inflatable tanks. Greek interpreters were recruited and the Allies stockpiled Greek maps and currency. Radio traffic concerning troop movements was generated from Cairo, while the headquarters of the invasion of Sicily in Tunis confined its communications, as much as possible, to landlines.

Earlier in the war, naval intelligence had suggested dropping a corpse at sea carrying misleading papers on it to deceive the enemy. The origin of the idea seems to have been the assistant to the director, Lieutenant Commander Ian Fleming, the creator of James Bond. The suggestion was taken up by Flight Lieutenant Charles Cholmondeley, who had been seconded into MI5 and was secretary to the XX (or Double Cross) Committee that dealt with double agents. He was assisted by Lieutenant Commander Ewen Montagu from naval intelligence.

They hatched a plot where they would drop a corpse in the sea off Spain carrying documents indicating that invasions of Greece and Sardinia were planned with only a diversionary attack on Sicily. Only a month before, a plane transporting a British officer carrying top secret documents and a French agent from Britain to Gibraltar had crashed into the sea off Cádiz and information had been passed to the Germans.

They approached the celebrated pathologist, Sir Bernard Spilsbury. He assured them that the Spanish, being Catholic, were particularly averse to conducting post-mortems. Besides, as a corpse began to decay, the lungs naturally filled with fluid which it would be hard to distinguish from seawater.

Next, they had to find a corpse. With a war on, the coroner for the Northern District of London said: 'I should think bodies are the only commodities not in short supply at the moment [but] even with bodies all over the place, each one has to be accounted for.'

Clearly there were legal difficulties involved. The deceased must not have any living relatives who would claim it for burial or cremation.

Eventually, a suitable body was found. It belonged to a homeless Welshman named Glyndwr Michael, who had died from eating rat poison. Montagu said he was 'a bit of a ne'er-do-well, and that the only worthwhile thing that he ever did he did after his death'.

His body would he dressed in a Royal Marines uniform, as any information would be passed back to the Admiralty and, hence, naval intelligence. He was to be Captain (Acting Major) William Martin. His rank was high enough to be carrying top secret papers, but low enough for there not to be any publicity if he went missing. His name was chosen as there were a number of officers around his rank in the Royal Marines named Martin.

His uniform would be easy to obtain, but there was a problem with the identity cards and passes that he would have to carry. Clearly, if he had been in the service for some time, they could not be new, so they were issued as replacements for lost originals. Photographs had to be taken of an MI5 officer who looked like Michael when he had been alive. Plainly, a picture of the dead man would be no good. Montagu then buffed the results up on his trousers to make them look used.

The documents he would be carrying in a briefcase chained to his wrist would contain a letter from General Sir Archibald Nye, the vice chief of the Imperial General Staff, to General Sir Harold Alexander, commander of the Anglo-American 18th Army Group in Algeria and Tunisia, ordering reinforcements needed to assault Greece and Crete as the Germans seemed

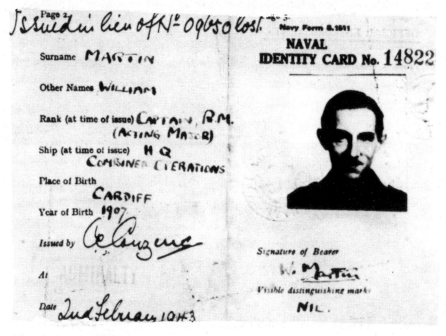

The identity card for 'Major Martin' – the man who never was.

to be building up their defences there. It also mentioned Sicily and the Dodecanese as 'cover targets'. Though confidential, this message was below the level of secrecy that would have required encrypted transmission.

These orders were accompanied by a letter of introduction from Martin's purported commanding officer, Vice-Admiral Lord Louis Mountbatten, the chief of combined operations, to Admiral of the Fleet Sir Andrew Cunningham, the commander-in-chief of the Mediterranean Fleet, saying that Martin was on loan until the assault was over. It also contained a quip about sardines that Montagu hoped the Germans would see as a reference to a planned attack on Sardinia.

If Martin was to be convincing, he would be carrying other things in his wallet and pockets. He would carry a book of stamps, a silver cross and a St Christopher's medallion, cigarettes, matches, the stub of a pencil, keys and a receipt for a new shirt. A back story also had to be provided. In his pocket would be a photograph of an MI5 clerk posing as his fiancée Pam, along with two love letters from her, a receipt for an engagement ring, a letter from his father and one from his bank concerning an overdraft. The ink had to be tested to see how well it stood up to being soaked in seawater. Added to that, there would be ticket stubs from a London theatre and a bill for four nights' lodging at the Naval and Military Club, plus other items he might have picked up while staying in London from 18–24 April.

The body was to be dropped off the port of Huelva in southern Spain, where it would be found by local fishermen. It was known that there was a very active agent for the *Abwehr* in the area, and also the British vice-consul in the city was reliable. The plan was signed off by Churchill. The approval of Eisenhower, who was commanding the invasion of Sicily, was also sought.

The idea of simulating a plane crash was considered too risky, so the body was packed in an airtight canister packed with dry ice to prevent it decaying too much without freezing it. That would have been easy to detect. The canister was loaded on to a submarine at Greenock in Scotland. From there, it was taken to the Mediterranean. The crew of HMS *Seraph* were told that the canister contained meteorological instruments.

The submarine surfaced off the coast near Huelva at 4.15 am on 30 April 1943. The canister was opened and the body was lowered into the water. The wash from the submarine's propellers then gently pushed it towards the shore.

Around 9.30 am, local fishermen found the corpse, which was then handed in to the authorities. They reported the discovery of the body and the briefcase to the British vice-consul who, in turn, contacted the Admiralty. Using a code that the British knew the Germans had broken, the Admiralty replied that it was vital for the vice-consul to retrieve the briefcase as the contents were important.

After a brief post-mortem which concluded the victim had drowned, the body was buried with full military honours. The vice-consul laid a wreath on behalf of Martin's father and fiancée. The briefcase was sent to Madrid, where the *Abwehr* put pressure on the authorities to examine the

The officers on board HMS Seraph *responsible for dropping the body so that it would float ashore.*

contents. The documents were removed from their envelopes by inserting a probe under the flap and rolling them up. The narrow tube of damp paper could then be removed without damaging the seals.

The documents were then flattened, dried and photographed. The copies were then sent to Germany. The letters were rolled up again and reinserted into their envelopes. These were then soaked in seawater again before the briefcase and its contents were handed over to the British vice-consul, who sent them to London in the diplomatic bag.

Although the envelope and the contents appeared untampered-with, a single eyelash that had been inserted with the letters in each envelope was missing, showing that the documents had been removed and read.

A cable in the code the British knew the Germans had broken was sent, telling the British naval attaché in Madrid that the envelopes had not been opened and the contents were secure. To further convince the Germans of the veracity of the documents, a notice of Major William Martin's death on active duty appeared in *The Times* on 4 June 1943. By chance, the notice appeared alongside those of two real naval officers who had died in an aircraft accident reported in the newspaper earlier. Alongside the list was a report of the death of the British film actor Leslie Howard, who had been on board a civilian aircraft shot down over the Bay of Biscay.

The Royal Marines were informed that 'no action is to be taken in respect of the death of Major William Martin', as he had been on secret secondment. Meanwhile, the fishermen who had discovered the body and the briefcase were given a reward of £25 – a princely sum in Huelva in 1943 – as the British were, apparently, so relieved to have the documents returned.

But the Germans had already swallowed Mincemeat hook, line and sinker. Hitler had ordered the battle-hardened and re-equipped 1st Panzer Division to move from France to Greece and told Mussolini that he must defend Sardinia and Corsica at all costs. The German troop strength on Sardinia was doubled to more than 10,000, supported by additional fighter aircraft. German torpedo boats were transferred from Sicily to the Aegean. Rations and fuel earmarked for Sicily were diverted.

After Operation Husky, the invasion of Sicily, began on 9 July 1943, Hitler continued to believe that it was a feint. Four hours after the invasion began 21 aircraft left Sicily to reinforce Sardinia.

Still convinced that the main attack would come in the Balkans, two armoured divisions on the Eastern Front were put on alert to head south. Between March and July 1943, the number of German divisions in the Balkans increased from eight to 18, in Greece from one to eight, and Erwin Rommel was sent to Salonika to prepare the defence of the region.

In Operation Husky, nearly half a million Allied troops faced 300,000 of the enemy defending 965 km (600 miles) of coastline. The Italian forces – largely Sicilian conscripts, the old and unfit, poorly equipped and ill-trained – largely disappeared after the US government made a deal with convicted gangster Lucky Luciano for the Mafia to step in.

The Allies completed the invasion of the island in under six weeks. The Italian dictator Mussolini was deposed and imprisoned. The new government began negotiations with the Allies. Hitler called off his offensive at Kursk. His defeat there was the beginning of the end on the Eastern Front, particularly because German troops had to be diverted to Italy after the capitulation of its Fascist government.

BODYGUARD, FORTITUDE AND PHANTOM ARMIES

The problem with D-Day and the Allied invasion of northern France was that the Germans knew that the Allies were coming. Even though it seemed self-evident that they would attack sooner or later, the western Allies actively encouraged the notion. In Operation Cockade, British intelligence fed information to the Germans that the Allies intended to attack somewhere along the Atlantic coast. The idea was to force the Germans to tie up German men and munitions in western Europe, relieving pressure on the Red Army in the east while Allied forces were fighting their way up the Italian peninsula from the south.

The central ploy for Allied intelligence was to keep the Germans thinking that the Allies would take the shortest Channel crossing and the landings would come at the Pas de Calais, rather than in Normandy, so they would concentrate their forces there. This would be difficult, as the Germans already knew that the British were masters of deception, thanks to Operation Mincemeat only a year earlier that had led the Germans to expect an invasion of Sardinia, with a diversionary attack in Greece, rather than the landings that came in Sicily.

Consequently, Allied intelligence officers were asked to keep a close watch on the Pas de Calais to make sure that the Germans were still building up their strength there. The Allies also needed to know that there was a minimal amount of activity in Normandy. If the Germans were ready and waiting, as they had been at the disastrous raid on Dieppe in 1942, the landings in Normandy in Operation Overlord had the potential of turning into the biggest military catastrophe the world had ever seen.

When it came to deception, the British still had a couple of tricks up their sleeves. First there was Ultra. This was the codebreaking system developed by Bletchley Park that deciphered top-level German military communications encrypted in the Enigma code, which the Germans still thought was unbreakable. Bletchley Park was able to tell the intelligence officers spreading disinformation whether their deception was working on the enemy.

Aiding the Allies was the rivalry between the *Abwehr*, military intelligence and the *Sicherheitsdienst*, or *SD*, the intelligence wing of the *SS* and the Nazi Party. The head of the *SD* – and author of the 'final solution' – Reinhard Heydrich aimed to take over the *Abwehr* and get rid of its chief, Admiral Wilhelm Canaris, who was a known anti-Nazi. After Heydrich was assassinated in Prague in 1942, *SS* chief Heinrich Himmler also sought to get rid of Canaris, but the admiral had evidence that Himmler had a Jewish grandmother, so the *SS* could not move against him directly. However, Canaris was sacked by Hitler for being a defeatist in February 1944 and replaced by *Oberstleutnant* Georg Hansen, who, it turned out, would be one of the 20 July conspirators.

In an attempt to increase their influence over Hitler, the rival groups within German intelligence inflated their estimates of the enemy's strength, leading the *Führer* to believe that the Allies had between 85 and 90 divisions available for the invasion. In fact, they had just 35. This played into the hands of Allied counterintelligence, which flooded the airwaves with messages concerning the non-existent First United States Army Group and the equally mythical British Fourth Army.

Radio intercepts about these fictitious armies were backed with reports from German spies in Britain who had been turned. This was easy to organize, as all Nazi attempts at espionage in the UK were extraordinarily inept. The Germans sent agents to Britain who could not speak English fluently and who knew nothing about the country. They were supposed to mingle with the large population of foreigners who had fled Nazi persecution. But the areas where the invasion force was being mustered were closed to foreigners and they were easily picked up. Most never got that far. They were arrested on the beaches. Many were eager to give themselves up.

In March 1944, Joseph Jan Vanhove, a German agent claiming to be a leading figure in the Belgian Resistance, turned up at the British embassy in neutral Sweden. He was on the run, he said, and the Germans had put a price on his head. To prove his story, he produced newspaper cuttings from the German-controlled Belgian press showing his photograph. This immediately alerted the British. What genuine resistance fighter on the run would carry incriminating newspaper cuttings with him as he fled across occupied Europe? He was flown to Scotland, where he was released to see if he would lead MI5 to other contacts. When it was clear that he was working on his own, he was arrested. Notes on shipping movements and bomb damage were found on him. These were enough to earn him a death sentence at his trial in the Old Bailey on 26 May 1944.

Before World War II, the Germans had installed two spy organizations in the UK. One was a network of domestic servants. They were to report back anything of importance they heard or saw, but their main role was as a screen to distract the attention of MI5 and Scotland Yard's Special Branch from the professional agents of the *Abwehr* operating in the country. Before they were despatched to Britain, the *Abwehr* sent their agents to a special school in Hamburg where they were trained to look and behave like Englishmen. Their instructor, an Oxford graduate, told them that their best cover was to create an aura of respectability – and respectability in Britain depended on having a healthy bank balance. He taught his spies to open a Post Office savings account when they arrived in Britain and deposit all the *Abwehr* funds they had brought with them in it. Then they should go to the police and report the loss of the account book, mentioning how much was in it. This, he said, would be enough to convince the police that they were respectable citizens. However, the instructor was an MI6 plant. On the day war broke out, the British police had a list of practically every *Abwehr* agent in the country.

Key to the British counterintelligence operation was a Canadian called Snow. He was an electrical engineer, but he fancied himself as a spy. First, he offered his services to British naval intelligence in 1936; later, he approached MI6. Both turned him down. So he offered his services to the *Abwehr*. MI5 had naturally been keeping an eye on him and, the day after war was declared, he was picked up. It was suggested to him that he might like to become a double agent. As his only alternative was a long drop at the end of a short rope, he agreed. Snow was in radio contact with the *Abwehr* and his handlers in Hamburg regularly informed him of agents they were sending. He passed this information on to the British authorities and they, too, were picked up.

The Germans had more success in occupied France, where they could pick up British agents and members of the French Resistance, or *maquis*. As D-Day approached, the Allies had to tell the *maquis* of their plans so that they could coordinate the assault with the sabotage activities of the Resistance and minimize civilian casualties. German intelligence in France discovered the date of the invasion this way. But the prime task of German intelligence operations in France was to track down and kill the Resistance, not to interrogate them, and the information they had was lost in the fog of Allied deception.

Even though the Red Army was moving in relentlessly from the east and the Allies were moving inexorably up the Italian peninsula, Hitler was still convinced he could win the war. With his secret weapons – the V-1 and his London Guns that could shell the capital from the coast of France – he believed that he could pummel Britain into surrender. Although the Allied bombing campaign was taking its toll, especially on the Luftwaffe, war production had increased tenfold since 1940 and there was no crisis of supply. Hitler had tanks and guns that were superior to anything the Allies possessed, and an army of 10 million battle-hardened troops.

Jet fighters were coming into service that could out-fly any Allied plane and the V-2 – the first modern ballistic missile – was in production. To prevent London being turned into a heap of smoking rubble, the Allies would have to take out the launching sites in the Pas de Calais. This was another reason Hitler was convinced that the Allied assault would come there and why it was protected by the strongest sector of the Atlantic Wall, Germany's coast defences that ran from the Arctic Circle to the Spanish border. Behind it, he kept his most powerful defensive force, the awesome Fifteenth Army.

It was very much in the interest of the Allies to let Hitler go on believing this and a massive deception operation was set in action. The overall plan to deceive the Germans in World War II was called Operation Jael, after the Old Testament story of the wife of Heber the Kenite, who persuaded the commander-in-chief of the Canaanite army that he was safe in her tent then, when he was asleep, drove a tent peg through his head. The deception plan surrounding D-Day was called Bodyguard, after a remark by Churchill at the Tehran Conference, between Churchill, Roosevelt and Stalin, in November 1943, where Stalin agreed to launch an eastern offensive to coincide with the Normandy landings. Churchill said: 'In war time, truth is so precious that she should always be attended by a bodyguard of lies.'

Bodyguard itself consisted of two parts: Zeppelin and Fortitude. Zeppelin was the operation to convince the Germans that the threat lay to the south or southeast. There was a real danger to the Reich in this area. Since the failure of the German invasion of Russia, Hungary had tried to change sides and both Bulgaria and Romania were trying to pull out of their treaties with the Axis powers.

Zeppelin tried to convince Hitler that there would be an Anglo-Soviet invasion of Romania from the Black Sea, an Anglo-American assault on Trieste and a British attack on the Balkans through Greece. From there, the Allies would move on through central Europe and Austria into southern Germany. Key to Zeppelin was the so-called 'Cicero Affair'. A Turk named Elyesa Bazna, codenamed Cicero, told the Germans that he had obtained the keys to the despatch boxes in the British embassy in Ankara. He photographed the contents and passed over copies of highly classified secret documents. At first, there was some doubt in the minds of German intelligence about whether 'Cicero' was a plant, but the Germans became convinced when the British began to make a fuss about security at the embassy. Bazna was all the more convincing as it appears he was a genuine spy. But his activities were known to British intelligence and, unbeknownst to him, the despatch boxes were seeded with misinformation. As a result, Hitler reinforced the Balkans with 25 divisions that could have been in France on D-Day.

The other leg of the campaign of deception, Operation Fortitude, had three parts. Fortitude North tried to convince the Germans that the invasion was coming in Norway. Sweden, until then neutral, would come into the war on the Allied side. This would allow the Allies to land in occupied Denmark and attack northern Germany. Fortitude South sought to confirm the idea in Hitler's mind that the attack would come in the Pas de Calais or on the coast of Belgium. Then there was Fortitude South II, also known as Rosebud, which continued after D-Day. This was largely a radio operation designed to convince the Germans that the D-Day landings were merely a feint and that the real invasion of the Pas de Calais was still to come.

Bodyguard was directed at Hitler personally. As the war progressed, he took more control away from his generals and exercised absolute authority from his fortified headquarters at Berchtesgaden in Bavaria and, chiefly, the Wolf's Lair at Rastenburg in East Prussia. He never went to the front or visited bombed cities, preferring to run his campaigns from maps and seeing no one but a handful of staff officers. So, if a campaign of deception convinced Hitler that was all that mattered.

The thrust of the campaign was to make Hitler believe that if the Allies were going to invade France, they could not do so before July 1944, so the attack was more likely to occur in the Balkans or Norway. The idea was to get him to disperse his forces around the perimeter of his empire. And Hitler fell for it. As Field Marshal Gerd von Rundstedt, commander in the west, said, the 'Bohemian corporal', as he contemptuously called Hitler, would try to hold on to everything and so, in the end, would lose everything.

The Allies played on Hitler's growing paranoia. He was to be led to believe that he was hemmed in on all sides by his enemy and would never know where or when they would attack. He was also led to believe that when the invasion of France came, the main force would strike across the Straits of Dover at the Pas de Calais, though there would be diversionary attacks elsewhere – on the Calvados coast of Normandy, for example. It was vital that, even after the Allies had committed everything to the beaches at Normandy, Hitler keep his Fifteenth Army in the Pas de Calais, waiting for an invasion there that would never come. Using Ultra, the Allies could see just how well their deception plans were working.

Although Hitler relied solely on his own intuition, Rundstedt's more objective analysis of the situation also led him to conclude that the Allies would strike at the Pas de Calais. As the Straits of Dover offered the shortest cross-Channel route, there could be a quicker turnaround of landing craft and, thus, a quicker build-up of the beachhead. The Allies could give an assault force there maximum air cover. As planes were spared a long flight from their airfields in England, they could spend longer over the battlefield. The Pas de Calais also offered the shortest route to the main objective – Germany itself. Rundstedt reckoned that, if the Allies made a successful landing in the Pas de Calais, it would take them just five days to reach the Rhine with a catastrophic effect on the morale of the *Wehrmacht* and the German people. On the way, the Allies could destroy the sites of the new weapons that were threatening London, and there was every chance that they would seize at least one major port intact.

Knowing that the possession of a port would be vital to any invasion, Rundstedt ruled out the possibility of an attack on Normandy. The two harbours there, Cherbourg and Le Havre, were bristling with demolition charges. If an invasion fleet attempted the 160 km (100 mile) crossing from the English coast, it was bound to be spotted by radar, reconnaissance aircraft or German high-speed E-boat patrols. By the time the invasion fleet reached the Normandy coast, demolition charges would be fired and the ports put out of action. However, if the Allies made a dash across the Straits of Dover, they might be able to capture Calais, Dunkirk or Boulogne before the Germans had time to blow up the port facilities.

Admiral Theodor Krancke, commander of the German Navy Group West, also believed that the Allies would have to land near a large port.

After studying Allied amphibious landings, he believed that beach obstacles and coastal defences could hold them off. Any attack would have to come at night at high tide, he thought, so that the landing craft could sail over the obstacles. An attack would have to be mounted away from cliffs and reefs where there might be awkward cross-currents, in conditions were the swell was less than 2 m (6.5 ft), with wind speeds of no more than 48 km/h (30 mph) and visibility of at least 4,500 m (14,764 ft).

Rommel disagreed. He believed that the Allies would have to land at low tide in daylight, so that engineers could blast any beach obstacles out of the way. But he, too, thought that the Allies must seize a major port. This had never been the Allies' intention. As early as June 1938, British combined operations planners had considered the idea of floating piers. General Dwight D. Eisenhower, who would become supreme commander of the invasion force and later president of the United States, recalled that when the idea of a floating 'Mulberry' harbour was first raised at a joint planning meeting in 1942 it was greeted by 'hoots and jeers' by the Americans. Despite this initial reaction, the Americans came round and the floating harbour was to become a reality – though, admittedly, other methods were tried. First, there was a plan to build a breakwater by sinking old ships filled with concrete, until it was discovered that only ships with a large draught could land supplies at the rate required. So even the biggest sunken ships in the makeshift breakwater would be well below the incoming supply ships, making unloading difficult.

There were also experiments to create a 'calm area' where ships could be unloaded by creating a curtain of bubbles using compressed air. This was abandoned in favour of the Mulberry harbour, which was tested successfully in Scotland in June 1943. Two were then built – one for the British sector and one for the American. They were designed to withstand gales of up to force six on the Beaufort scale, last for 90 days and deliver 12,000 tonnes of cargo to shore each day, whatever the weather. The American Mulberry failed to do this because it was put together in too much of a hurry, without proper soundings being taken, but it did well enough. Interrogation of captured German commanders after the invasion

A Mulberry harbour off the coast of Normandy in 1944.

revealed that the Germans knew nothing of the Mulberry harbours. This gave the Allies a huge advantage. Bringing their own harbours with them meant that they could attack at any place along the coastline, giving them the element of surprise.

Operation Bodyguard was also designed to keep vital operational plans, such as the deployment of the Mulberry harbours, secret. It was run by a secret office inside Churchill's headquarters called the London Controlling Section, under Colonel John Bevan and Lieutenant Colonel Sir Ronald Wingate. They worked closely with 'C', the head of MI6, the counterintelligence organization MI5 and a special sector of MI5 called the XX (Double Cross) Committee. The job of the XX Committee was to turn German agents. As all the German spies in Britain were picked up almost immediately, the XX Committee had plenty to choose from. Likely candidates were then subjected to lengthy interrogations by a special team in Battersea. To be a good spy, an individual needs to be resourceful and self-reliant – which implies a certain independence of mind. This meant that dedicated Nazis did not make good spies. They were handed over to the civilian authorities for trial. Thirty of them were found guilty and executed.

However, the XX Committee found that most of the agents recruited by the *Abwehr*, and not a few recruited by the *SD*, had grave misgivings about Nazism. After the German defeats at El Alamein and Stalingrad, it seemed Hitler was not so invincible after all and these agents became increasingly easy to turn. As double agents, they were a potent weapon in feeding false information to Hitler. And as they were in contact with their handlers in Germany, the British knew what information was being requested. This, too, gave them a powerful insight into the mind of the enemy.

The false information fed to German intelligence by double agents was backed by radio intercepts picked up by KONA, the German Signal Intelligence Regiment, which tuned into all Allied radio traffic. Obviously, this had to be done subtly, with the utmost skill. If information came too easily, the enemy would smell a rat. Fortunately, Ultra told the Allies which of their codes the Germans had broken. These could be used to drop snippets of false information to the Germans which backed up what their agents were telling them. The Allies even used bursts of messages from a specific area, which KONA could identify with its direction-finding equipment, in codes the Germans had not broken, to give the impression that there was a troop build-up there.

Due to the differing frequency of traffic among the various tiers of an army – at corps, division and brigade levels – it was possible to create in the German mind an entirely fictitious order of battle. As the RAF controlled the skies over Britain, German reconnaissance aircraft were only allowed to see what the Allies wanted them to see. And German agents on the ground in Britain could confirm vital parts of the picture that German intelligence meticulously built up from the disinformation fed to them.

Newspapers were another important source of sending disinformation to the enemy as major British newspapers were often available in neutral countries. Clippings from the local press could also be sent via a neutral country to German spymasters. Provincial newspapers were a particularly good means of spreading deception. They often included information about local men and women who were in the services, mentioning in passing their unit and their whereabouts. Engagements and marriages of service personnel filled the announcement columns and the letters pages carried complaints from local people protesting about the rowdy behaviour of men from a unit billet in the area. By placing fictitious stories, personnel ads and letters according to a meticulous plan, a huge counterfeit canvas could be painted.

When America entered the war, the head of the FBI, J. Edgar Hoover, who was profoundly anti-British, would have nothing to do with the XX Committee. But after the establishment of the Office of Strategic Services, the forerunner of the CIA, under Major General 'Wild Bill' Donovan in 1942, America set up the Joint Security Control (JSC), which mirrored the London Control Section, and Hoover created America's own XX Committee, known as X2. JSC and X2 ran a similar disinformation campaign in the US. During the planning of the Normandy invasion the Anglo-American strategy of deception was co-ordinated by the Joint Committee of Special Means.

Even though J. Edgar Hoover had no time for the British, he was no slouch when it came to counterintelligence. Even before America entered the war, he had a complete list of German agents working in the US (and a less complete one of the British agents operating there). Like the British, he was aided by the ineptitude of German intelligence. Agents were sent who had no real command of English. In one particularly amateurish operation, eight German agents were sent to sabotage American factories. It was called Operation Pastorius.

Before the German agents went, they took leave in Paris. Their drunken conversations were overheard by the Resistance and details of their mission were passed on to MI6, who forwarded the information to the FBI. During this leave, one member of the party contracted a venereal disease and was unable to continue. On board the U-boat that was to land them surreptitiously on the eastern seaboard, they were given American money. This had been captured in the Pacific and some of it had been overprinted in Japanese. The rest was in old bills that were no longer legal tender. Once ashore, two of the German agents gave themselves up immediately and offered their services to the American government. Another, who was rather more dedicated, went into a drugstore to buy a razor and, through force of habit, clicked his heels, raised his arm in a Nazi salute and bellowed, 'Heil Hitler'. He was promptly arrested.

The rest of the saboteurs were rounded up, tried, convicted and sentenced to death, though the two men who had given themselves up had their sentences commuted. In 1948, they were granted executive clemency and deported to the American sector of West Germany.

However, not everything was plain sailing. After the fall of Canaris (see page 172), suspicion fell on a British double agent, known as Artist, who was an *Abwehr* officer working out of Lisbon. He was kidnapped by the *SD*, drugged and smuggled back to Germany, where he was interrogated by the Gestapo in their notorious Prinzalbrechtstrasse headquarters in Berlin. Artist had been recruited by Dusko Popov, a Yugoslavian playboy and MI5 double agent in the *Abwehr* (and a man many think James Bond was based on). He was a gambler who passed messages by the numbers he bet on in the casino in Estoril. Once, Popov was gambling in Lisbon when he was annoyed by a Lithuanian who would call '*Banque ouverte*' every time he held the bank, indicating there was no upper limit. Popov pulled out $30,000, which belonged to MI5. The Lithuanian blanched and declined the bet. Popov put the money back in his pocket and walked away.

This incident became part of the Popov legend. Ian Fleming, the author of the James Bond books, was in naval intelligence at this time and would have known about Popov. He could well have given Bond some of Popov's attributes.

Popov was a legendary womanizer. His disinformation operation was called 'Tricycle', because of his fondness for taking two women to bed at the same time. He also had an affair with French actress Simone Simon.

In August 1941, Popov discovered that the Japanese were preparing to attack Pearl Harbor. He informed the FBI, but bureau chief J. Edgar Hoover dismissed the information – possibly influenced by his mistrust of all things British, including their double agents. He discovered that Popov had taken

Dusko Popov – playboy and double agent thought to be a model for James Bond.

a woman with him from New York to Florida and threatened to have him arrested under the Mann Act if he did not leave the US immediately.

If, under torture, Artist had given up Popov and the rest of his ring, the whole of Fortitude South would have been blown. Through Ultra, the Allies heard that Hitler had moved several reserve formations into Normandy. The D-Day planners held their breath. But Artist did not talk. He either died under interrogation or was summarily executed and the all-important Fifteenth Army stayed east of the Seine.

As part of Fortitude North, the headquarters of a non-existent British Fourth Army was set up in Edinburgh, ready to decamp for Scandinavia at any time. In fact, the headquarters was just a handful of radio operators, sending out messages that the Germans would pick up. Others were deployed in Stirling and Dundee. Their radio traffic was so convincing that a German plane was sent to bomb the Dundee outpost. Meanwhile, two German double agents, codenamed Mutt and Jeff, reported the arrival of a Russian liaison officer. Part of the plan fed to the Germans was that the Red Army would be making a simultaneous thrust through Finland. The Russian had been sent to co-ordinate the Soviet part of the operation with the British Fourth Army and a small contingent of the fictitious American Fifteenth Army, stationed in Northern Ireland, that had also been ostensibly earmarked for the invasion of Norway.

Messages from this outfit gave the Germans the impression that it was a two-corps headquarters, with an armoured division, an airborne division and four infantry divisions. There were references to equipment and training in rock-climbing, skiing and other cold weather operations, along with details of sporting fixtures and social events.

As part of Fortitude North, Allied agents in Norway were asked for detailed information about the conditions and defences there. Even when this was done in codes that the Germans had not broken, the increase in radio traffic between Scotland and Norway convinced them that something was about to happen there. Even the Soviets got in on the act, leaking disinformation about the mustering of an army ready for an assault on Scandinavia and naval preparations for an attack on the Finnish Arctic

Sea port of Petsamo, then occupied by the Germans. Indeed, in June, the Red Army really did attack Finland, a wartime ally of Germany until the summer of 1944, as part of its offensive in the east to coincide with the D-Day landings.

German intelligence naturally wanted confirmation that there was an army mustered in Scotland. It contacted its two most reliable agents in Britain – Dusko Popov, and a Spaniard known as Garbo. Both confirmed a military build-up north of the border. Reconnaissance planes were sent over, which the RAF let through. They saw numerous planes were on Scottish airfields – dummies made out of wood and canvas – and lochs were full of Royal Navy warships. These were real, but they were not destined for Norway. They were part of Task Force 'S', which would head for Sword Beach in Normandy on D-Day.

To complete the picture, an Anglo-American military mission was sent to neutral Sweden to investigate the possibility of moving troops down to the Baltic. Air reconnaissance was increased. Commando raids along the Norwegian coast were stepped up. Factories, communication centres and railways were sabotaged. The volume of radio traffic to Norwegian and Danish Resistance groups also grew. And shipping was attacked, resulting in fatal damage to the German battleship *Tirpitz* and the sinking of the troop ship *Donau* and a number of merchant vessels. The clinching piece of evidence, in the minds of German intelligence, was an entirely erroneous report of a visit by the British Foreign Secretary Anthony Eden to Moscow, supposedly to conclude the plans to invade Scandinavia. Hitler became so convinced that the Allies would attack in Norway that he kept nearly 500,000 Germans with their artillery, tanks and air support who could have been in France tied up in Norway for the rest of the war. When the Allies eventually turned up in Scandinavia, the war was over and 372,000 men surrendered with hardly a shot being fired.

Meanwhile, the fictitious US First Army Group was mustering in southeast England ready for its landings on the Pas de Calais. News of its existence was first supplied by the FBI though a triple agent, a Dutchman named Albert van Loop. A member of the *Abwehr*, he had been sent to

Madrid where he approached the US embassy and offered to work for the OSS or the FBI. To prove he was genuine, he handed over two ciphers, his call sign and various security checks.

The FBI was aware that he was still working for the Germans, but figured that he could be useful to them anyway. He was shipped to New York, where an American agent used the material he had provided to impersonate him. Information was then sent about real US Army units being shipped across the Atlantic for D-Day whose presence in England was bound to surface in the press anyway. Van Loop, unaware that he was being impersonated, also sent messages of his own, but due to the confusion surrounding the *SD*'s takeover of the *Abwehr*, this did not alert anyone in Germany to the deception. When the FBI found that the Germans believed the impersonator, they began feeding him information about the fictitious US First Army Group. In Britain, MI6's double agents and all the other methods perfected by the London Controlling Section and the XX Committee were used to confirm its existence. The deception was so effective that Garbo was paid £20,000 by the Germans to run a non-existent spy ring dedicated to spying on the US First Army Group.

The Spaniard Garbo was a fanatical anti-Nazi who had approached MI6 in Madrid early in the war. But as he was Spanish, MI6 felt it could trust him. However, the *Abwehr* took him on. From Lisbon, using maps, newspapers and guidebooks, he began manufacturing fictitious reports from a non-existent network of three agents on his own account. When MI6 discovered that the German Navy was combing the high seas for a non-existent convoy travelling from Liverpool to Malta that Garbo had made up, they recruited him and brought him to London, where he expanded his network to 14 non-existent agents. The Germans trusted him so much that they informed him every time that the key of their Enigma traffic between Hamburg, Madrid and Tangiers was changed, saving Bletchley Park a great deal of time working out the new key for themselves.

Another important agent in the disinformation campaign was Brutus, a Polish intelligence officer who had helped get the first Enigma machine to Britain before the war. When Poland was invaded, he escaped to Paris and worked for MI6. He was betrayed to the *Abwehr* who were, themselves, looking for enemy agents they could turn. He agreed to work for them, provided that the 100 MI6 agents the *Abwehr* had already captured were treated as prisoners of war, rather than executed as spies. The *Abwehr* agreed and sent him to Madrid. From there, he travelled to London and offered his services to MI6 once more. However, the XX Committee was reluctant to use him as the *Abwehr* knew that he had worked for MI6 before. Nevertheless, they seemed to trust him and he fed them information that he said he had gleaned in his new job as liaison officer between the RAF and the Polish Air Force.

A fourth agent used in Fortitude South was a French woman called Treasure. She had joined the *Abwehr* to get out of occupied France. They sent her to Britain, via Spain. In Madrid, she went to the British embassy and was taken to London, where she was vetted by the XX Committee. She told the *Abwehr* that she had joined the Auxiliary Territorial Service – the women's branch of the British Army. Later, she told her handlers that she had begun an affair in Bristol with an officer in the Fourteenth Army, part of the fictitious US First Army Group. When she reported that the Fourteenth Army had been moved to Essex, ready for the invasion of the Pas de Calais, its presence there was verified by signal traffic incepted by KONA, the German Signal Intelligence Regiment. Another clinching detail was that someone in Geneva began buying up all the Michelin maps of the Boulogne-Lille area. Hitler was all the more convinced that the main assault would come across the Straits of Dover when KONA overheard that General George S. 'Old Blood and Guts' Patton had been appointed commander of the First Army Group.

The Luftwaffe increased its aerial reconnaissance over southeast England. They saw tracks indicating that tanks and other armoured vehicles were being hidden in the woods there. Other tanks were parked in plain sight. Landing craft were moored in the creeks and estuaries and, in Dover, what looked like a large oil refinery was being built to supply petrol to the invasion force. None of these were real. Special effects men and set builders and been recruited from theatres and movie studios to fool German aerial reconnaissance. They developed special track-making machines and made inflatable Sherman tanks, which looked like the real thing from the air. The landing craft were made out of plywood and canvas and the oil refinery in Dover was one huge movie set.

Although as far as the Germans were concerned, the First Army Group was under the command of Patton, the fictitious invasion of the Pas de Calais was not going to be an exclusively American operation. The British Twenty-first Army under General Montgomery was in on it too. His headquarters for the real invasion of Normandy were in Portsmouth, but its radio traffic was relayed by landline to a transmitter in Kent. So, in the build-up to the real invasion, KONA, the German Signal Intelligence Regiment German Y Service, saw a dramatic increase in traffic from the very area an invasion force heading for the Straits of Dover would muster.

An inflatable tank – these looked real to German reconnaissance.

Hitler bought this story completely, but Rommel was not so sure. He had been pitted against Montgomery in the deserts of North Africa and knew his tactics and his use of deception. He figured that the Allies were giving the impression that they had more divisions than they actually did. If he was right, there would only be one invasion, not three – one in the Balkans, one in Norway and one in France. The build-up of men and materiel in England led him to believe that it would come in France.

To break through the Atlantic Wall, the Allies would have to concentrate their forces on one small area to punch their way through. In Rommel's inspection of the Atlantic Wall from Dunkirk to Biarritz, he ascertained that the best place to attack was in Normandy. He figured that the invasion would come just after daybreak, at low tide, preceded by airborne landings. This meant that he was prepared for landings on 5, 6 or 7 June, depending on the weather. But he could not shake from his mind the idea that the Allies had to take a port in order to succeed. Cherbourg and Le Havre would be out of action by the time the invasion fleet appeared over the horizon. And he wondered how the Allies would give their landing force adequate air cover more than 160 km (100 miles) from their air bases. Nevertheless, Rommel appealed to Hitler to move four of his Panzer divisions to the west, ready for an attack on the Normandy coast. Hitler refused. He remained convinced that the invasion would come in the Pas de Calais. Besides, his armoured reserves in the west were low due to Operation Zeppelin. The Allied military planners followed the messages being sent back and forth between Rommel and Hitler with interest via Ultra. They learnt that, as a result of Hitler's intransigence, only two under-strength, poorly equipped and thinly spread divisions, who had to use horses and mules to move guns and supplies, were left to defend the Normandy beaches between Cherbourg and Le Havre.

Only one of the Allied deception operations seems to have failed. It was called Operation Copperhead and involved Montgomery's double – an actor named Clifton James. He appeared in Gibraltar, ostensibly to organize an invasion of the south of France. The Spanish dictator General Franco was also asked whether he would allow Barcelona to be used as the base for the evacuation and treatment of Allied wounded. This was naturally reported back to the Germans. Unfortunately, while Montgomery was a well-known teetotaller, James got very publicly drunk and the operation was cancelled. Ironically, an Allied invasion of the south of France did take place. On 15 August 1944, the US Seventh Army and the French First Army landed on the Riviera. Operation Copperhead having failed, there were only four German divisions to oppose them.

Although Rommel could not convince Hitler to move Panzers into Normandy, he directed his attention to strengthening the beach defences there. In May 1944, Allied air reconnaissance spotted a build-up of the defences and obstacles along the Calvados coast. The German Sixth Parachute Regiment was moved into the landing area, and the Ninety-first Air Landing Division, which specialized in anti-paratroop operations, moved into the Cherbourg peninsula and occupied areas that were going to be the drop zones of the 82nd and 101st US Airborne divisions. These had to be moved but, as the drops had to mesh with the rest of the Overlord plan, they could not be moved far. Suddenly, it seemed that Fortitude had been blown. In fact, Hitler had spotted that there was a weak point along the Normandy coast and had moved his troops to cover it. Maybe this was his much-vaunted intuition coming into play. But he still believed that the attack was coming in the Pas de Calais so he kept his Panzers to the east of the Seine.

Admiral Krancke, using his faulted analysis of the situation, calculated that the invasion would definitely come on 18 May. When it did not, he forecast that it would come in August. Meanwhile, von Rundstedt studied the pattern of Allied bombing in May. When he noticed that they were taking out the Seine bridges, he began to think that the Allies might make a landing in Normandy. But if they did land in Normandy, he believed that they would have to land on the Cherbourg peninsula itself because of their need for a port. Even then it would only be a minor or diversionary attack. He still agreed with Hitler that the Allied main force would land in the Pas de Calais.

Even though the Germans had strengthened their defences in Normandy, things were still looking very favourable for the Allies' landings there. Then, with just a week to go before D-Day, the Germans moved up the battle-hardened German 352nd Infantry Division. Direct from the Russian front, they would be responsible for the slaughter of American troops landing on Omaha beach. The story is told that the Resistance group who reported their presence communicated with their British handlers via carrier pigeon and the pigeons carrying the message were shot as they passed over the coast. If this is true, the pigeon message was only a back-up. Information that the 352nd Infantry was in Normandy did reach London, but the D-Day planners did not tell the men landing on Omaha beach of their presence in case it had an adverse effect on morale.

In late May 1944, while troops of a dozen different nationalities disappeared from the pubs and shops of rural England and began mustering silently at the embarkation points, Operation Fortitude went into overtime. Radio traffic from Patton's fictitious US First Army Group was stepped up. While vehicles in full black-out moved to the embarkation ports, others with not too carefully hooded lights moved back and forth along the roads of southeast England.

These movements were accompanied by a volley of reports from the XX Committee's double agents concerning troops movements in Kent and East Sussex. To add to the confusion, a new double agent, a young woman codenamed Bronx, told her German handlers that she had definite information that the landings would be in the Bay of Biscay on 15 June. Treasure then reported that she had made friends with the girlfriend of General Marie-Pierre Koenig, commander of the Free French, who had told her that the invasion would come on the Pas de Calais in the second week of July.

In all, 250 messages were sent, each giving a different date and place for the invasion – including one from the French officer in Algiers saying that the invasion could come in Normandy on 5, 6 or 7 June. The officer may have been a triple agent working for the Germans, or London Controlling Section may have felt that if this possibility was overlooked, the Germans may have drawn their own conclusions. Shifting though the incoming messages, the new head of the *SD* Walter Schellenberg concluded that the French officer was right, the invasion would come in Normandy on 5, 6 or 7 June. But by that time the number of conflicting reports had left the reputation of German intelligence in tatters and Schellenberg's conclusion led the German High Commander to believe that the invasion would come anywhere but on the coast of Normandy and on any day except 5, 6 or 7 June.

Admiral Krancke's belief that the invasion would definitely come on 18 May proved a godsend. Throughout May the weather was hot and dry and the sea was calm. It was perfect invasion weather and the German defenders grew tired of constant alerts, followed hours later by stand downs. The troops in Normandy were doubly tired because of Rommel's ceaseless efforts to strengthen local defences. By the first week of June, everyone needed some sleep.

As sunny day followed sunny day and the Allies still did not come, scepticism spread. The defenders began to believe that the Allies were not going to invade at all. It had all been a huge ruse. The British and Americans, it was felt, were going to bide their time in England, in safety on the other side of the Channel, and let the Russians do all the work – or postpone any invasion until the Germans were forced to take their troops away from the Atlantic Wall to defend the eastern border of the Fatherland.

With no sign of a seaborne landing coming crossing the Channel, there was a hiatus on the other fronts. In Italy, the Allies drew back from the fight as they prepared their push to link up with their landings at the Anzio beachhead and advance on Rome, while the Russians were preparing their summer offensive that was timed to coincide with the D-Day landings. Suddenly, in this quiet period, there were hundreds of Commando raids knocking out German radar and radio-interception stations in Norway, Denmark, Rhodes, Crete and the Balkans, again deceiving the Germans as to where the invasion could come.

France, itself, seemed to be more dangerous than the Russian front as the Resistance began to take revenge on the occupiers. Factories and fuel-dumps were blown up. Trains were derailed and individual soldiers returning to their billets at night disappeared without trace. The German reaction was to slaughter any members of the *maquis* they caught. Otherwise, they took their revenge on innocent citizens. This provoked revulsion and hatred among the French people and the Resistance was soon recruiting more people than it lost.

Even Hitler began to think that the Allies' invasion preparation might all have been a hoax to distract his attention from the Eastern Front. Something had to be done to convince him that the attack across the Pas de Calais was about to go ahead. Information about the imminent invasion must come from an unimpeachable source. It was decided that the former head of the *Afrika Korps*, Panzer General Hans Kramer, who held the Knight's Cross of the Iron Cross, with Oak Leaves, would make a suitable messenger. Since his capture in North Africa, Kramer had been held in a prisoner-of-war camp in south Wales, but he was in ill health and the Swedish Red Cross had organized his repatriation in May 1944. On his way out of the country, he was given a seemingly accidental tour of ports full of shipping, airfields with their endless ranks of aeroplanes and bustling army assembly stations – though he was told that they were in Kent and East Sussex when they were, in fact, in Hampshire. The signposts had been removed from British roads in 1940 in the hope that it would disorientate invaders, so there was nothing to give the game away. Everything Kramer saw, apparently, belonged to the US First Army Group. With the courtesy due to his rank as a general, Kramer was introduced to the commander-in-chief of the First Army Group, General Patton himself. He also enjoyed an informal chat with Patton's senior officers, who left him in no doubt that they were heading for Calais.

Kramer returned to Germany on the Swedish vessel *Gripsholm*, arriving on 23 May. His debrief once again convinced the Germans that the invasion was on. His reports of the Allied strength spread alarm and despondency. Göring even accused him of being a defeatist. The Germans went back on the alert once more. But they still had the same old problem. No one knew when or where the invasion would come – though Kramer had confirmed Hitler's view that the Pas de Calais was the place to watch.

General Hans Kramer – a prisoner-of-war who was exchanged to unwittingly take false information to the Germans.

It is not as if the Germans did not have their opportunities to find out the truth. Sergeant Thomas P. Kane, an American soldier of German descent in the Ordnance Supply Section of Supreme Headquarters in London, sent top-secret documents to his sister in Chicago by mistake. The authorities were alerted when the parcel burst open in an Illinois sorting office. Although the explanation was innocent enough, Kane, his sister and everyone in the sorting office who might have seen the documents, was kept under strict surveillance until after D-Day.

Another breach of security came when a British staff officer left a briefcase containing the communication plan for Operation Neptune, the naval part of Overlord, in a taxi. Fortunately, the driver handed it in immediately at the Lost Property Office. At the beginning of June, an old army friend of General Eisenhower announced in the dining room of Claridge's that the invasion would come before the 15th. He was demoted and sent back Stateside. Another American officer was also repatriated after getting drunk at a party and revealing top-secret information.

But the worst scare came when eight tank landing craft were sunk by German E-boats while rehearsing for D-Day in Lyme Bay. Some 650 men were killed or drowned. Among them had been several 'Bigots' – the codename given to personnel who had been cleared to see invasion information at the highest level. Two of the E-boats had sailed slowly among the survivors and one of them was seen to switch on its searchlight as if looking for something. It was not beyond the bounds of possibility that prisoners had been taken. Divers were sent out to retrieve identity tags from the corpses. Eventually, all of the missing 'Bigots' were accounted for.

On the eve of D-Day, German signals intelligence worked out that all the RAF stations that were readying themselves for action were in southwest England, far from the Pas de Calais. This indicated that the attack would come in Normandy, but they could get no one in the High Command to listen to them. Hitler distrusted signals intelligence on principle. Their report merely led him to believe that a diversionary attack would be staged in Normandy. The level of radio traffic from the US First Army Group

– which Kramer had now seen – convinced him that the attack was still coming across the Straits of Dover.

Nevertheless, as D-Day approached, the Allies were on tenterhooks. A senior British officer who did the crossword in the *Daily Telegraph* every morning discovered that Omaha and Utah – the codenames of the two landing beaches in the US section – along with the words Overlord, Neptune and Mulberry came up in a series of five crosswords between 2 May and 2 June. Could undetected German spies be using the *Telegraph* crossword to send messages to Berlin? MI5 investigated. They discovered that the crosswords were compiled by two schoolmasters in Leatherhead, Surrey. The senior compiler had been doing the job for 20 years; the other was an old friend. Even though they had supplied the crosswords some six months in advance – before some of the codenames had even been thought up – they were subjected to the most stringent security checks and seemed genuinely distressed during their interrogation. The investigation gave them a clean bill of health, though the Americans were still sceptical.

Associated Press, in London's Fleet Street, actually announced the invasion on 3 June. A 23-year-old teletype operator who had been working on a dry run for an invasion special accidentally ran the tape. News desks on five continents read the news: 'URGENT PRESS ASSOCIATED NYK FLASH EISENHOWER'S HQ ANNOUNCES ALLIED LANDINGS IN FRANCE.' The mistake was rectified quickly enough to prevent the story being carried in any newspaper, but the news did reach both New York's Belmont Park racetrack and the Polo Grounds, where the New York Giants were playing the Pittsburgh Pirates. At both venues the crowds, at the announcers' request, rose to offer a silent prayer for the Allies' success.

General Eisenhower himself was considered a security risk because, with his wife left back in America, he was having an affair with the ATS driver Kay Summersby, an Irish divorcee. This could have left him open to blackmail. Although Ireland was neutral during the war – and many men from the Republic fought valiantly for the Allies – many there harboured anti-British sentiments.

Churchill was another security risk as he spent a lot of time on the phone to Roosevelt. Ultra showed that the Germans were intercepting their calls and a new scrambler was installed in February 1944. However, from the length and frequency of the calls, Schellenberg somehow deduced that the invasion would come in France, not in the Balkans as Zeppelin implied.

The greatest invasion secret of all was the one hardest to conceal – the Mulberry harbours. They were to be secured by huge concrete caissons, the size of apartment blocks. They were too big to be hidden or camouflaged and they were spotted moored off Tilbury by German reconnaissance planes. The Germans even seemed to know what they were for. On 21 April 1944, the radio propagandist William Joyce, known as Lord Haw-Haw for his sneering tone of voice, said: 'You think you are going to sink them on our coasts in the assault. We'll save you the trouble. When you come to get under way, we're going to sink them for you.'

As D-Day approached, fear spread through Supreme Headquarters. If the Germans had figured out about the Mulberry harbours, they would know that the Allies did not need to take a port with the first assault and there were few places along the coastline where floating harbours of sufficient scale could be deployed. Was it merely a coincidence that the Normandy beaches were being reinforced? Ultra came to the rescue again. The Japanese ambassador to Berlin, Baron Hiroshi Baron Oshima, sent regular reports back to Japan which were intercepted and decoded. The Allies found these very useful. In October 1943, he had toured the whole of the Atlantic Wall and sent a long, detailed report that was of more interest in Washington and London than it was in Tokyo. In April 1944, he toured the Wall again and was given a detailed briefing by General von Rundstedt. In it they discussed the huge caissons that the Luftwaffe had seen at Tilbury. Von Rundstedt had come to the conclusion that they were anti-aircraft gun towers. Hitler himself believed them to be replacements for harbour moles and jetties that might be destroyed by demolition charges or in an assault and only strengthened his view that the Allies were going to seize a major port. Bodyguard and the Mulberry secret were safe.

At the beginning of June, aerial bombardments of the inland targets began. But because the Germans were trying to install more V-1 launch ramps in the woods and forests of the Pas de Calais there was enough bombing in that area for the Germans to continue to believe that was where the assault would come. Meanwhile, the defenders of the Atlantic Wall were complacent due to Krancke's statement that the invasion would not come now until August. The general feeling was that any attack would coincide with a Russian offensive. In the east, the thaw had come late that year and the Red Army would not be able to move until the end of June at the earliest. And when the weather began to change over France and the Channel, it was thought that the Allies had missed their chance. Even Krancke began to believe that the whole thing was a hoax and that Kramer had been deceived.

Rommel took the opportunity to brainstorm possible responses to an Allied landing. Once again he realized that it was vital that the Panzers were moved west of the Seine and put under his control. Once the Allies had gained a foothold, he believed, the only way they could be defeated was in a big set-piece battle which could only be won by a commander on the spot – not one hundreds of kilometres away in Rastenburg. Hitler had repeatedly refused to hand over command of the Panzers. Rommel began to believe that the only way he could be convinced was to go and see the *Führer* personally.

Had the weather stayed fine, there was no way he would have left his headquarters in Normandy. But at the beginning of June it showed signs of breaking. Rommel's wife's birthday was on 5 June. He planned to pay a flying visit home, then go on to Hitler's headquarters where he had arranged a meeting with the *Führer* on 6 June. By then Rommel was the only senior officer who still believed that the invasion was still coming. But that only led him to make another major mistake. Fearing air raids, Rommel had removed the guns from their emplacements in many places along the Wall. During his assessment of the Wall, he had noted that they lacked the necessary 4 m (13 ft) of concrete to protect them from bombing. The guns would be safe enough as they were kept nearby and well camouflaged. He believed that he would have at least 24 hours' warning of any attack, which would give his men plenty of time to put them back. But the defenders in Normandy did not get 24 hours' warning of the invasion. When it came, Rommel was not even in France to order the guns' return.

On 1 June a storm began to blow up. Nevertheless, Eisenhower set the date for the invasion as 5 June. The forecasts got worse and, by 3 June, he postponed it until 6 June. One convoy of 140 ships, carrying the US Fourth Infantry Division, was already on its way and out of radio contact. If they arrived at the beaches alone, without support, there would be a massacre. A plane was sent which dropped a canister containing a message telling them to turn back. It fell in the sea. The pilot scrawled a second message on his knee, put it in another canister and, this time, managed to hit the deck of the commodore's ship. After what seemed like hours, the convoy turned back towards the English coast.

Everything now depended on the weather. At a pinch, they could delay until 7 June. Otherwise, they would have to wait 14 days until the tides were right again and the men and equipment were now already aboard the invasion fleet. They would have to disembark, return to their assembly areas and go through the whole embarkation procedure again two weeks later. This, it was thought, would have a disastrous effect on morale.

Then, on 4 June, Eisenhower's chief meteorologist, Group Captain John Stagg, spotted a lull in the storm. Between the afternoons of Monday 5 June and Tuesday 6 June the weather would be calm enough for Operation Neptune to go ahead. It was a huge risk. Weather forecasts are never that accurate. The air chiefs, Air Chief Marshal Sir Trafford Leigh-Mallory and Air Chief Marshal Sir Arthur Tedder, were worried about the flying conditions. But Eisenhower and Montgomery were both ready to take a chance. They knew that bad weather would only add to the element of surprise. No one would expect the Allies to invade during a storm. They knew the Germans would know nothing of the lull in the storm that was approaching: the Allies had gone to great lengths in tracking down and destroying or jamming all the enemy's weather ships.

As the invasion plan got under way, Allied air strikes turned from targets inland to the coastal defences. German-occupied ports were mined and there was an increase in the coded messages being sent to the French Resistance on the BBC. But still the Germans thought it was a hoax and air reconnaissance revealed no build-up of landing craft in Dover harbour. As the weather closed in, patrols by German reconnaissance aircraft, E-boats and submarines were cancelled. The Germans were convinced that the weather made an invasion impossible.

To keep the Germans in the dark, the Resistance began cutting all telephone and telegraph wires, while three-men teams were air-dropped in to organize special operations. One group was captured and gave away the signal that would alert the Resistance that the invasion was on the way. The signal was a line from the poem *Chanson d'Autome* by Paul Verlaine. But when the line was broadcast repeatedly by the BBC, it was dismissed because of the bad weather. The defenders manning the Atlantic Wall in the Pas de Calais went on the alert later, while those in Normandy took leave, attended parties, wrote letters home, or simply slept.

On the night of 5–6 June, as Operation Neptune went into action, all Allied intelligence could to do was monitor German radio traffic. Ultra picked up nothing untoward and, as far as anyone could tell, the Germans had no idea what was about to happen. Meanwhile, another piece of D-Day was going into action. Lancaster bombers dropped chaff – strips of radar reflecting metal – at precise intervals across the Straits of Dover. They also used an electronic device called Moonshine, which gives enemy radar operators multiple images of a plane, making a handful of aircraft look like a huge squadron. Then, launches towing barrage balloons carrying radar reflectors set out into the pitching sea. Soon, radar operators on the Pas de Calais saw what appeared to be a huge fleet covering an area of some 518 sq km (200 sq miles) coming their way. While in Normandy there was no alert and no German gun fired until the invasion fleet appeared over the horizon, in the Straits of Dover search lights swept the waters, coastal batteries opened fire and naval units put to sea to find… nothing at all.

There was one final bit of deception to come just a few minutes after midnight on 6 June – D-Day itself – when hundreds of dummy paratroopers were dropped. When they hit the ground they set off detonators that simulated the sound of small arms fire. Flares, smoke canisters, mortar bombs and machine gun simulators were also dropped. These were aimed at wooded areas where it would be difficult to know what was going on. But it appeared that a full-scale airborne assault was in progress and battle was raging on the ground. These dummy assaults even drew some of the defenders of Omaha beach away from their positions, which meant the slaughter there was not quite as bad as it might have been.

The assault troops were now on their way. With them they carried detailed maps of what confronted them. Eisenhower said that it was unlikely that any army had ever gone into battle better informed. The Allied intelligence-gathering operation had been a complete triumph. So had the deception plan, which continued after the landings. Hitler held back his

The D-Day landings would have been a failure if Operation Fortitude had not fooled the Germans.

Fifteenth Army in the Pas de Calais, awaiting the non-existent US First Army Group until long after the Allies had broken out of their beachhead. Hitler himself, it has been said, was the most valuable weapon in the Allied armoury. Believing himself to be a military genius, he stayed away from the battle front, directing the fighting from his Wolf's Lair where he could be deceived by tricks as old as war itself.

ADMIRAL CANARIS

While Admiral Canaris perished after the 20 July plot, he had been conspiring against Hitler as head of the *Abwehr* for ten years. During that time, as well as working against Hitler's best interests, he had clandestine communications with the British. But, make no mistake, Wilhelm Canaris started out as a fanatical Nazi.

He joined the German Imperial Navy in 1905. At the outbreak of World War I, he was a naval intelligence officer on board SMS *Dresden*, a light cruiser that evaded the Royal Navy in the Battle of the Falkland Islands in December 1914, largely because of Canaris' skilful evasion tactics. Returning to Germany, he worked in naval intelligence, finishing the war as a U-boat commander.

After the war, he helped organize the anti-Communist *Freikorps* and was a member of the military court that tried and in many cases acquitted those involved in the murders of the leftist revolutionaries such as Rosa Luxemburg.

When Hitler came to power in 1933, Canaris was on board the battleship *Schlesien*, where he gave the crew lectures about the virtues of Nazism. He was an enthusiastic supporter of the new regime even after the Night of the Long Knives.

He said: 'We officers … should always recognize that without the *Führer* and his NSDAP, the restoration of German military greatness and military strength would not have been possible … the officer's duty is to be a living example of National Socialism and make the German *Wehrmacht* reflect the fulfilment of National Socialist ideology. That must be our grand design.'

In January 1935, Canaris was made head of the *Abwehr*. This put him in a guarded rivalry with Reinhard Heydrich, head of the *SS* intelligence service, the *Sicherheitsdienst*, or *SD*. Canaris regarded Heydrich as a 'brutal fanatic', while Heydrich saw Canaris as a 'wily old Fox' and monitored the *Abwehr*'s telephone traffic.

In 1936, Canaris and Heydrich signed an agreement sharing counterespionage responsibilities between the *Abwehr* and the Gestapo, which had also come under Heydrich's remit. Meanwhile, Canaris was promoted to rear admiral and expanded the staff of the *Abwehr* from 150 to almost 1,000. He remained a committed Nazi and an anti-Semite, and was the first to suggest that Jews should be forced to wear the Star of David.

During the Spanish Civil War, Canaris used contacts he had in Britain's Vickers armaments company to supply arms to General Franco and the Nationalists. Before the *Anschluss*, he personally oversaw deception operations designed to give the impression that Germany was planning an armed invasion. In Vienna, he used this as a cover to seize records from the Austrian archives that revealed his connections to Britain and Vickers during the Spanish Civil War. He also absorbed as much of the Austrian intelligence service into the *Abwehr* as he could while avoiding taking on any hardline Nazis.

For Canaris, the *Anschluss* concluded the establishment of the 'Greater Germany'. But he and his deputy General Hans Oster then began to have their doubts about Hitler's ambitions. They were afraid the annexation of the Sudetenland and Czechoslovakia would lead to another European war. (Hans Oster was the leading light of a 1938 conspiracy devised to storm the Reich Chancellery, kill Hitler and dismantle the Nazi Party if it looked as though war would break out over the Sudetenland Crisis; when Britain backed down over the issue and allowed Hitler to continue with his invasion, the assassination plan was abandoned.) With conservative politician Ewald von Kleist-Schmenzin, Canaris had his own, less radical plan. It was to stage a putsch to unseat Hitler.

Wilhelm Canaris, head of German military intelligence, who secretly worked against Hitler.

Kleist contacted MI6, who agreed that the German invasion of Czechoslovakia would lead to war. It was agreed that if Britain declared war, the conspirators would seize the opportunity to overthrow Hitler in the name of the peace-loving German people who had suffered terribly in a disastrous war just 20 years earlier. However, as with Oster's more violent plan, the Munich Conference gave the Sudetenland to Germany and Hitler took over the rest of Czechoslovakia without resistance. The moment was lost.

Oster survived for the time being, but in 1943 he was placed under house arrest after *Abwehr* officers were caught smuggling Jews out of Europe. After the 20 July plot, Canaris' diaries were seized. They revealed Oster's long-term anti-Nazi activities and he was executed in April 1945.

In January 1939, Canaris manufactured the 'Dutch War Scare'. The British government was led to believe that the Germans were about to invade the Netherlands and use the Dutch airfields to launch strategy bombing raids to raze British cities. As a result, Prime Minister Neville Chamberlain promised to send troops to France if it was attacked.

After the outbreak of war, Canaris visited Poland and saw Warsaw in flames. 'Our children's children will have to bear the blame for this,' he said. He also witnessed the war crimes committed by the *Einsatzgruppen SS* teams behind the lines who shot Jews and anyone considered politically undesirable. In Będzin, he saw the burning of the synagogue with 200 Polish Jews inside and he received reports from *Abwehr* agents about other incidents of mass murder throughout Poland.

Canaris went to see Hitler to complain, but the chief of the *Oberkommando der Wehrmacht* (OKW, Supreme Command of the Armed Forces), Field Marshal Wilhelm Keitel, warned him not to, saying that orders for the atrocities had come directly from the *Führer*.

With his subordinate, General Erwin von Lahousen, Canaris attempted to form a circle of like-minded *Wehrmacht* officers in 1940, with little success. After the failure of Operation Pastorius, Lahousen was sent to the Eastern Front, where he joined Tresckow's attempt to kill Hitler. Wounded, he was out of commission when the 20 July plot failed and lived to testify against *Reichsmarschall* Hermann Göring and others at the Nuremberg War Crimes Trial.

Canaris had further objections to the harsh treatment of Soviet prisoners of war and the summary execution of Soviet commissars, but again Keitel advised him to hold his tongue. This was not a 'chivalrous war', Keitel said, it was 'a matter of destroying a world ideology'. Heydrich noted Canaris' squeamishness and marked him down as 'politically unreliable'.

When Spanish dictator General Francisco Franco refused to come into the war on Germany's side because Hitler refused to let him have the French territories in North Africa, Canaris was sent to see Franco to persuade him to let German troops pass through Spain to take Gibraltar – otherwise he would invade. Franco wanted Gibraltar for himself and, contrary to Hitler's orders, Canaris persuaded him not to allow German troops to pass though, lest he provoke the British into attacking Spain.

Franco need not be afraid of a German invasion, Canaris said, revealing the secret plans for Barbarossa – the German invasion of the Soviet Union. With that in progress, Germany would not have the strength to invade, let alone garrison, Spain. Franco should not help Germany until Britain was defeated. As a result, Spain stayed out of the war completely.

Through his mistress Halina Szymanska, a Polish spy based in Switzerland, Canaris also told the Allies of Barbarossa. The intelligence was passed to Stalin, who did not believe it.

After 1942, Canaris visited Spain frequently and was probably in contact with British agents from Gibraltar. He also made contact with British agents in occupied France. On one occasion he asked what peace terms Germany could get if they got rid of Hitler. Churchill's reply was 'unconditional surrender'.

Canaris also determinedly kept his organization out of the persecution of the Jews, training some of them as *Abwehr* agents and giving them false papers. He was later recognized as a Righteous Gentile by the Yad Vashem Holocaust memorial.

But it couldn't go on. At the behest of Heinrich Himmler, Canaris was dismissed and the *Abwehr* disbanded. He was placed until house arrest, only to be released to coordinate the resistance to the Allied blockade. He was arrested again on 23 July 1944 after 20 July plotter Georg Hansen alleged that Canaris was the 'spiritual instigator' behind the plot. Though no concrete evidence was produced against Canaris, his diaries implicated him in the conspiracy. Canaris was tried for treason before an *SS* summary court, convicted and sentenced to death. He was hanged from a butcher's hook on 2 April 1945, less than a month before the end of the war in Europe.

THE BATTLE OF LOS ANGELES

'Searchlights and Anti-aircraft Guns Comb Sky During Alarm' ran the headline of the *Los Angeles Times* on 26 February 1942. At around 1.45 am the night before, the newly deployed coastal radar picked up a blip from an unidentified aerial target 193 km (120 miles) west of Los Angeles. It was heading straight for the city.

By 2.15 am, two more radar sites confirmed the contact, and at 2.25 am the city's air raid warning system went off. Then the shooting began. The city, it seemed, was under attack by the Japanese.

Less than three months earlier, the Japanese made a surprise attack on Pearl Harbor, the US Navy base on Honolulu, killing 2,403 Americans and badly damaging the US Pacific Fleet. Until then America had managed to stay out of World War II, which had largely been confined to Europe, North Africa and the Atlantic.

Japan, Germany and Italy then declared war on the US. Congress responded. America was now at war.

Americans had seen the bombing of European cities and the London Blitz. With the Pacific Ocean now, apparently, the playground of the Japanese Imperial Fleet, air attacks on the American mainland were on the cards. Los Angeles seemed to be a prime target. Much of the US Pacific Fleet lay at anchor in San Pedro Bay. The shipbuilding industry there employed 22,000 and it was a centre of aircraft production.

Five hundred US Army troops had been moved into the nearby Walt Disney Studios complex in Burbank to defend the factories in case of an invasion. Bunkers were built. Radar installations and anti-aircraft batteries were deployed, ready for the attack that Angelenos feared would come.

Japanese submarines were already in action along the coast of California. On 23 December 1941, they sank the oil tanker *Montebello*. The next day, they attacked the lumber ship SS *Absaroka*. Other merchant ships were sunk, damaged or harassed. For Californians, the war that had been on the other side of the world was coming close to home.

Then, on 23 February 1942, the Japanese submarine *I-17*, captained by Kozo Nishini, sailed into the Santa Barbara Channel and began firing on the facilities at Ellwood Oil Field 16 km (10 miles) up the coast from Santa Barbara. This was the first naval bombardment of the continental United States by a foreign power since the Royal Navy shelled Baltimore in 1814.

Though little damage was done, the attack sparked an invasion panic among an American populace not used to dealing with war on the home front. At the time, there was little in the way of defences. So Angelenos were on the alert the following night when the sky in a 63 km-long (39 mile) arc from Santa Monica to Long Beach was lit with searchlights, tracer bullets and the flashes of exploding shells.

At 7.21 am the regional warning centre finally issued an all-clear and the clean-up began. The incident had indirectly resulted in five casualties, three killed in car accidents that happened during the blackout, and two by heart attacks caused by shock. Anti-aircraft batteries had fired off some 1,430 rounds, none of which hit an enemy aircraft.

In the immediate aftermath, the US Army and US Navy disagreed about what had actually happened. Secretary of War Henry L. Stimson claimed as many as 15 enemy aircraft had flown over Los Angeles, while Navy Secretary Frank Knox said, 'As far as I know the whole raid was a false alarm … attributed to jittery nerves.'

His denial led to accusations of a cover-up. Some put the number of planes as high as 20, but given all the smoke in the sky from the anti-aircraft fire it would have been impossible to count accurately in any case.

The Army Chief of Staff General George Marshall told President Franklin D. Roosevelt that he, too, put the number at 15. Various speeds

Searchlights and Anti-aircraft Guns Comb Sky During Alarm

The Battle of Los Angeles newspaper report.

were reported from 'very slow' to 322 km/h (200 mph) and heights varied from 2,743 m (9,000 ft) to 5,486 m (18,000 ft). However, no bombs were dropped. There were no casualties among US troops. No planes were shot down and no American Army or Navy planes were involved.

'Investigation continuing,' Marshall reported. 'It seems reasonable to conclude that if unidentified airplanes were involved they may have been from commercial sources, operated by enemy agents for purposes of spreading alarm, disclosing location of anti-aircraft positions, and slowing production through blackout. Such conclusion is supported by varying speed of operation and the fact that no bombs were dropped.'

Other theories abounded – that the Japanese had a secret airbase in Mexico, or that they had developed submarines that could carry planes, or the whole thing had been staged by the US government to prepare the American people for war.

Congressman Leland M. Ford of Santa Monica called for a Congressional investigation, speculating: 'This was either a practice raid, or a raid to throw a scare into two million people, or a mistaken identity raid, or a raid to lay a political foundation to take away Southern California's war industries.'

The attack, he feared, would justify moving the factories further inland and out of his constituency.

There were other consequences. Some reported seeing flashing lights during the raid, as if Japanese spies were signalling to shipping. The following day Japanese Americans living on Terminal Island near Los Angeles Harbor were told they had 48 hours to leave their homes.

Execution Order 9066 authorizing the internment of Japanese Americans had already been signed on 19 February 1942, six days before the so-called Battle of Los Angeles. The implementation of it was quickly speeded up. Over 120,000 Japanese Americans were rounded up and sent to concentration camps in the Midwest. In California, anyone with one-sixteenth or more of Japanese blood was incarcerated.

At the end of the war, the Japanese government declared that they had flown no airplanes over Los Angeles during the war. In 1983, the US Office of Air Force History concluded that meteorological balloons had been the cause of the initial alarm.

Later in the war, the Japanese did send balloons carrying bombs on the jet stream with the intention of starting forest fires. This failed, but six people in Oregon were killed by one of the bombs, the only war fatalities on the continental United States.

Also in 1983, the Commission on Wartime Relocation and Internment of Civilians issued a report saying there was little evidence of disloyalty among Japanese Americans at the time. In 1988, an official apology was issued and those who still survived were awarded $20,000 in compensation.

There is another conspiracy theory, though – that it wasn't a meteorological balloon that triggered the battle, but a UFO.

THE PHILADELPHIA EXPERIMENT

Merchant seaman Carl M. Allen claimed to have been serving on board the SS *Andrew Furuseth* in October 1943 when he witnessed an experiment in invisibility conducted by the US Navy in the Philadelphia Naval Shipyard – the so-called Philadelphia Experiment. According to Allen, the USS *Eldridge*, a destroyer escort ship, was made to disappear, leaving behind a mysterious green mist.

Further, the *Eldridge* somehow appeared in Norfolk, Virginia, then re-appeared in Philadelphia. Some of the crew went insane. Others were frozen in place, embedded in the fabric of the ship.

With World War II being fought on the waters of the Atlantic and the Pacific, camouflaging ships was vital to protect them from attack. The British had also been working on degaussing their ships, countering the magnetism induced in such a large body of steel to make them invisible to the sensors of magnetic mines or torpedoes, though the ship remained visible to the human eye, radar and underwater listening devices.

Degaussing was done by installing large electromagnetic coils. However, the equipment was expensive and another method called deperming was adopted. This involved a large cable carrying a heavy current being dragged along the side of the ship. But what Allen said he saw was much more sophisticated than that.

The story came to light in 1956, when Allen anonymously mailed a copy of Morris K. Jessup's book *The Case for the UFO: Unidentified Flying Objects* to the US Office of Naval Research (ONR). The book outlined

Jessop's ideas concerning flying saucers and alien races. It was annotated with handwritten notes in the margins, commenting on the author's conjectures. The notes purported to have been a discussion between three individuals, one of whom it was implied was an alien. Jessop, it seemed, was coming too close to revealing the military's advanced technology.

Two officers at the ONR took an interest and showed Jessup the annotated copy of his book. He noticed that the handwriting matched that of letters he had received from Allen, who sometimes used the pseudonym Carlos Miguel Allende. In them he gave details of the Philadelphia Experiment he had witnessed in 1943. He said that the incident had been reported in a Philadelphia newspaper, but the ONR could not find the story.

Making the *Eldridge* invisible was accomplished, Allen's letters said, by the application of Albert Einstein's 'unified field theory', which attempted to unify his general theory of relativity with electromagnetism. Einstein's earlier theoretical work had resulted in the atomic bomb, but his work on unified field theory was never completed. In 1943–44, Einstein was working as a part-time consultant with the Navy's Bureau of Ordnance, undertaking theoretical research on explosives and explosions, but there is no indication that he was involved in research relevant to invisibility or teleportation.

The ONR had only been established in 1946 and could not find any record of experiments in invisibility in 1943, or at any other time. It was concluded that the origin of the story may have been the routine experiments with degaussing that were undertaken in the Philadelphia Naval Shipyard.

There may also have been some confusion with experiments involving the destroyer USS *Timmerman*, which was fitted with a high-frequency AC generator which produced a current at 1,000 hertz rather than the standard 400 hertz. The higher frequency produced corona discharges, which sometimes had a blue glow. None of the crew suffered any ill effects from the experiment.

In a report published in 1996, the ONR said: 'In view of present scientific knowledge, ONR scientists do not believe that such an experiment could be possible except in the realm of science fiction.'

In 2017, the US Naval History and Heritage Command (NHHC) took another look, but could find no documents in the archives concerning the alleged event, or indicating any interest by the Navy in attempting such an outcome. The *Eldridge*'s log showed it was on convoy duty at the time. It was never in Philadelphia and only visited Norfolk briefly on 2–3 November 1943.

The SS *Andrew Furuseth* had left Norfolk for Oran on 25 October. It had been there since 4 October and had not visited Philadelphia either. The NHHC concluded: 'After many years of searching, the staff of the Archives and independent researchers have not located any official documents that support the assertion that an invisibility or teleportation experiment involving a Navy ship occurred at Philadelphia or any other location.'

However, Stealth technology has been developed since the alleged Philadelphia Experiment – and was probably being worked on then. Advances in the field, then and now, would not be widely publicized and archives can be selectively culled.

WHAT HAPPENED TO THE NAZI GOLD?

The Nazi state was essentially kleptocratic. It existed by stealing. The Jews were robbed of everything they possessed, right down to the gold in their teeth in the death camps. The Nazis stole some $550 million in gold from the governments of countries they overran, including $223 million from Belgium and $193 million from the Netherlands. That's a total of $10 billion at today's prices, excluding what they stole from individuals and private companies.

It is estimated that much of the looted money was passed through Swiss banks to neutral countries such as Portugal, Spain, Sweden, Turkey and Argentina, who provided vital war materials such as tungsten. More that 200 million Swiss francs' worth of gold coins is thought to have ended up the hands of the Vatican, though Catholic authorities deny this. The bulk of the remaining gold was held with the German reserves at the Reichsbank in Berlin.

During late 1944 and early 1945, as the bombing of Berlin increased and the Allies pushed toward the city from the east and west, much of the gold reserves was dispersed to banks in central and southern Germany. On 3 February 1945, the Reichsbank was hit, demolishing the building and destroying the presses for printing Reichsmarks. It was then decided that the gold reserves, worth some $238 million ($4.3 billion today), would be collected and hidden in a potassium mine near the town of Merkers in the German state of Thuringia.

Currency reserves totalling a billion Reichsmarks bundled in 1,000 Reichsmark bags, and a considerable quantity of foreign currency, was transported by rail to Merkers, where it was stored alongside artwork sent there for safekeeping. From 1942, the SS Office for Economy and Administration, which ran the concentration camps, stored the valuables stolen from the inmates there too, along with other looted goods.

Some jewellery was sold abroad and precious metals were melted down. At the last moment attempts were made to move the loot, but this was hampered by the speed of the Allied advance and bombing.

In early April 1945, American troops advancing into Thuringia found the potassium mine. At the base of the liftshaft that took them to the bottom of the mine, they found 550 bags of Reichsmarks, which the Germans had been attempting to move before being cut off by the US Third Army's advance. Further down the tunnel they found a huge steel vault door. The wall around it was blown by army engineers on 8 April.

Inside they found 8,198 bars of gold bullion; 55 boxes of crated gold bullion; hundreds of bags of gold items; over 1,300 bags of gold Reichsmarks, British gold pounds, and French gold francs; 711 bags of American $20 gold pieces; hundreds of bags of gold and silver coins; hundreds of bags of foreign currency; nine bags of valuable coins; 2,380 bags and 1,300 boxes of Reichsmarks containing 2.76 billion Reichsmarks; 20 silver bars; 40 bags containing silver bars; 63 boxes and 55 bags of silver plate; one bag containing six platinum bars; and 110 bags from various countries. In other tunnels, an enormous number of valuable artworks were discovered.

The find was inspected by the Supreme Commander of the Allied Expeditionary Force, General Dwight D. Eisenhower, Commander of the Third US Army, General George S. Patton, and Commander of the Twelfth US Army Group, General Omar Bradley. As the jittery lift descended with ever-accelerating speed down the pitch-black shaft, with a German lift attendant, Patton grew concerned about their safety. Looking at the single cable supporting the cage, he said if it snapped 'promotions in the United States Army would be considerably stimulated'. Eisenhower said: 'OK George, that's enough. No more cracks until we are above ground again.'

Bags of Nazi gold found in the mine at Merkers.

They were moved by what they saw.

'Crammed into suitcases and trunks and other containers was a great amount of gold and silver plate and ornament obviously looted from private dwellings throughout Europe,' Eisenhower wrote. 'All the articles had been flattened by hammer blows, obviously to save storage space, and then merely thrown into the receptacle, apparently pending an opportunity to melt them down into gold or silver bars.'

Patton recorded that he saw 'a number of suitcases filled with jewellery, such as silver and gold cigarette cases, wrist-watch cases, spoons, forks, vases, gold-filled teeth, false teeth, etc., acquired by 'bandit methods'.

Examining the stacks of Reichsmarks and the plates used for printing them, Bradley said: 'I doubt the German Army will be meeting payrolls much longer.'

Near the end of the inspection, Bradley said to Patton: 'If these were the old free-booting days when a soldier kept his loot you'd be the richest man in the world.' Patton just grinned.

The Americans had a problem. The find had been widely reported and Merkers would fall in the Soviet zone of occupation once the fighting finished. The booty was loaded on to trucks and transported to Frankfurt in two huge convoys with armed escorts and air cover.

The currency was returned to the countries it had been taken from and a commission was set up to restore the gold bullion to the various central banks. Efforts were also made to return the artworks and non-monetary precious metals to those they belonged to. But by no means had all the missing Nazi gold been discovered.

In the last months of the war, a train carrying 330 tonnes of gold, jewels, weapons and artworks was thought to have left Breslau (now Wrocław in Poland). It passed through the station at Freiburg (Świebodzice), but did not reach the next station at Waldenburg (Wałbrzych).

It was suspected that the train was sealed up in an abandoned coal mine or tunnel system under Książ Castle, part of the unfinished, top secret Nazi underground construction project in the Owl Mountains. After the war, Polish troops searched the area, but nothing was found.

In August 2015, two men named Piotr Koper and Andreas Richter said that they had found the train using ground-penetrating radar, which appeared to show a man-made shaft 50 m (164 ft) below the surface with something in it. The tunnel lay alongside Polish State Railways' Wrocław–Wałbrzych line.

The Polish authorities sealed off the area and the Polish Army cleared the woods, looking for mines and booby traps. None were found. Mining specialists scanned the area but could find no sign of the train, though they conceded that there may have been a collapsed tunnel underground.

Koper and Richter were not discouraged. With the help of private sponsors, they obtained the necessary permits and began digging. Several attempts have been made, but nothing has so far been found – leading some to conclude that the gold train never existed.

Although a gold train may not have existed in Poland, there was one in Hungary – or, at least, one that started out from Budapest. In mid-December 1944, as the Soviet Army began to encircle the Hungarian capital, a train of 42 wagons departed containing valuable possessions – ranging from Persian carpets to gold wedding rings and silver religious artefacts – that had been systematically plundered from Hungarian Jewry following the Nazi occupation of the country nine months earlier. It was headed for an 'Alpine redoubt' where the Nazis intended to make their last stand.

Along the way, more confiscated possessions were collected. The value of gold and other valuables was thought to be as much as $350 million ($6.4 billion today). Some was pilfered along the way. Árpád Toldi, the government official appointed by the SS to take the Jewish loot out of Hungary, made off with some. He succeeded in getting to Switzerland and subsequently disappeared.

After 14 weeks, the train arrived in Salzburg where it was seized by Allied troops, first by the French Army and then by the US Army. It was impossible to ascertain who most of the things belonged to, so they were sold off and the money was given to international refugee organizations.

PEARL HARBOR — WHO KNEW?

On 7 December 1941, Japan launched an attack on the American fleet at Pearl Harbor, bringing the United States into World War II. There is a conspiracy theory that the British knew in advance of the attack, but Prime Minister Winston Churchill did not tell President Franklin Delano Roosevelt as he knew it would bring the US into the war on the Allied side. Churchill had long held that beleaguered Britain could only withstand the Nazi onslaught with America as an ally.

On 18 May 1940, his son Randolph visited Churchill while he was shaving. His father had told him to sit down and read the papers while he finished. Randolph recounted the scene in his memoirs:

> I did as told. After two or three minutes of hacking away, he half turned and said: 'I think I see my way through.' He resumed his shaving. I was astounded, and said: 'Do you mean that we can avoid defeat?' (which seemed credible) or 'beat the bastards?' (which seemed incredible).
>
> He flung his Valet razor in to the basin, swung around, and said:– 'Of course I mean we can beat them.'
>
> Me: 'Well, I'm all for it, but I don't see how you can do it.'
>
> By this time he had dried and sponged his face and turning round to me, said with great intensity: 'I shall drag the United States in.'

But Churchill seems not to have known how this was to be done, other than build the closest possible personal relationship with Roosevelt. He does not seem to have known beforehand about the attack on Pearl Harbor. Rumours of a Japanese attack in Southeast Asia had been reported by Bletchley Park some days before the actual raid. The report had been shared with US intelligence, but the report was vague and assumed that the Japanese would invade Thailand. Both the US and the UK had underestimated Japanese intentions and capabilities and did not imagine that they might be capable of such a strategic surprise.

That Sunday, Churchill was noticeably depressed. Over dinner he was lost in thought and sometimes holding his head in his hands. Shortly before 9 pm Churchill's valet, Sawyers, brought in a portable radio so they could listen to the news. Churchill was a bit slow at switching it on and they missed the headlines. The first item the dinner party heard was about a tank battle in Libya.

The attack on Pearl Harbor – could it have been prevented?

Then the announcer returned to the lead story – that Japanese aircraft had attacked Pearl Harbor. Roosevelt had made an announcement, but the details of the attack were still sketchy. There was some argument among the diners at Chequers over whether the attack had been made on Pearl Harbor or the Pearl River.

Suddenly energized, Churchill slammed the top of the radio down. Sawyers re-entered the room.

'It's quite true,' he said. 'We heard it ourselves outside. The Japanese have attacked the Americans.'

Confirmation came from the British Admiralty. Churchill headed for the door, saying: 'We shall declare war on Japan.'

Chasing after him, dinner guest John Gilbert 'Gil' Winant, the American ambassador said: 'Good God, you can't declare war on a radio announcement.'

Winant then phoned Roosevelt to confirm the facts and said he was with a friend who wanted to speak to him, adding: 'You will know who it is as soon as you hear his voice.'

'Mr President', said Churchill, taking the phone. 'What's this about Japan?'

'It's quite true,' replied Roosevelt. 'They have attacked us at Pearl Harbor. We are all in the same boat now.'

'This certainly simplifies things', said Churchill. 'God be with you.'

Another version of this conspiracy theory is that Roosevelt knew of the attack and did nothing. Although he had won an election on the promise that he would not take America into the war in Europe, he had already signed the Atlantic Charter with Churchill which outlined their war aims. He also knew that, if Britain fell, the United States would be surrounded on three sides – by the Japanese dominating the Pacific and the Germans in the Atlantic, while many of the countries to the south were sympathetic to the Nazis.

In 1939, the Japanese introduced a new code whose decrypts the British and Americans called 'Purple'. It used a modified Enigma machine to encipher. This meant that Japanese had to be transliterated into the

Roman alphabet in what was called *romaji*. This made it easier to crack – at first using pencil and paper, then with an IBM tabulating machine and punch cards.

The whole process was speeded up when Purple was adopted by the Japanese Foreign Office. The diplomats tended to use standard phrases such as 'I have the honour to inform Your Excellency'. They liked to number paragraphs. Reading the Japanese newspapers also suggested the subject of the intercepts and the State Department often published the full text of diplomatic notes from the Japanese government that had earlier been intercepted when sent, enciphered, to the Japanese embassy in Washington, D.C.

Purple decrypts were circulated under the codename 'Magic'. Its circulation was restricted to the President, the Secretaries of State, War and the Navy, the Chief of Staff, the Chief of Naval Operations, the heads of the Army and Navy War Planning divisions and the heads of the Army and Navy intelligence divisions – ten people initially. Others did get to see the intercepts, but field commanders were specifically excluded. However, information from intercepts was fed to them, attributed to a 'highly reliable source'.

Soon, a dedicated Purple decoding machine was developed. Although America had yet to enter the war, it was decided that there should be a pact between the US and UK in the area of cryptography. This was the origin of the 'special relationship' which exists in intelligence matters to this day.

When American codebreakers, purporting to be a Canadian delegation, visited the British codebreaking centre at Bletchley Park, they took with them a Purple machine. In exchange, the British handed over Purple intercepts from the Far East Bureau in Hong Kong and, later, Singapore. The Purple machine the British had been given was sent there and, before the fall of Singapore, evacuated to Delhi.

A Purple decrypt of a message sent by Baron Hiroshi Ōshima, the Japanese ambassador to Berlin, reported that Hitler had told him that, 'in all probablility war with Russia cannot be avoided'. The US added its warning to those sent by Churchill to Stalin.

While the diplomatic code had been broken, the Japanese Navy code JN-25 – so called because it was the 25th navy code the Americans had identified – had not. Bletchley Park, the Far East Bureau in Singapore and the US Navy's cryptanalytic unit at Cavite Naval Base in the Philippines were all working on it. But just as progress was being made, the Japanese updated their codes as preparations for the attack on Pearl Harbor were underway.

In Hawaii, the US Combat Intelligence Unit worked on lesser codes concerning engineering, administration, personnel, weather and fleet exercises. A Purple machine was being made for them, but it did not arrive in time and was given to the British instead.

In July, the Combat Intelligence Unit overheard radio traffic leading them to believe that, in the wake of the fall of France, Japan was intending to take over the French colonies in Indochina – Vietnam, Laos and Cambodia. First, orders were sent from the commander-in-chief of the Japanese fleet to the forces in the south. Next, it appeared that personnel had been shuffled around. Messages for certain admirals had to be redirected. Then there was radio silence from the fleet. It was assumed the task force was underway. Messages were sent to it, but none were returned.

It was also noted that there were no messages to or from the aircraft carriers. It was assumed that these had been held behind in home waters, where communications would be by low-power, short-range transmission that would have died away before they reached US listening posts. American intelligence had seen this pattern before.

Efforts were also made to tap the phone and telegraph lines of the Japanese consulate in Hawaii. A young ensign there named Takeo Yoshikawa was sending back reports on the American ships in Pearl Harbor. On 4 December, he wired Japan's foreign minister, saying: 'At 1 o'clock on the 4th a light cruiser of the Honolulu class hastily departed.' This was sent, not in the naval code, but the diplomatic code that had already been broken.

US security was anything but tight. The German embassy in Washington reported to Berlin that the State Department had the keys to the Japanese codes. But just as the Germans thought that Enigma was unbreakable, the Japanese also believed that their codes could not be cracked.

The Americans had a problem finding enough Japanese translators who could pass the rigorous vetting process. Recruits had to have at least a year's experience in telegraphic Japanese, which was a language within a language. There was no punctuation and jumbles of letters had to be bunched together to made an ideograph.

In the autumn of 1941, as US–Japanese relations were reaching breaking point, American cryptographers were handling 50–75 messages a day, some as long as 15 typewritten pages. On at least one occasion, 130 messages had to be decrypted in a day. As negotiations between the US and Japan continued, these would have to be cracked, translated and rushed to the Secretary of State before the Japanese ambassador arrived to see him.

When the Japanese fleet set off, they left behind their regular radio officers to send seemingly routine messages in their familiar 'fists', easily recognized by American interceptors. The fleet itself proceeded in radio silence.

Meanwhile, the Americans were deciphering the diplomatic traffic. The US monitoring station at Bainbridge Island in Puget Sound then picked up a message informing Japan's Washington embassy to listen to the Japanese daily news bulletin broadcast on short-wave. If they heard the phase 'east wind rain', it meant US–Japanese relations were being broken off and they should destroy all code papers. 'North wind cloudy' meant there had been a rupture in relations with the Soviet Union, while 'west wind clear' meant the same had happened with the British. So there would be no mistake, the phrase would be repeated in the bulletin. Once this message was decoded by the Americans, monitoring stations turned their attention to short-wave broadcasts and the translators were soon overwhelmed.

On 20 November, the Japanese ambassador Kichisaburō Nomura presented an ultimatum to Secretary of State Cordell Hull, insisting the US abandon its support for China (where the Japanese had been fighting since 1937), allow the Japanese to make further conquests and provide them with as much oil as they needed. This was unacceptable to the Americans and a coded telephone message from the Japanese embassy in Washington, D.C., told the government in Tokyo that negotiations were getting nowhere.

Then a message from ambassador Ōshima in Berlin was intercepted. It told Tokyo that German Foreign Minister Joachim von Ribbentrop had assured him: 'Should Japan become engaged in a war against the United States, Germany, of course, would join the war immediately.'

Tokyo replied: 'Say very secretly to them that there is extreme danger that war may suddenly break out between the Anglo-Saxon nations and Japan through some clash of arms and add that the time of the outbreak of this war may come more quickly than anyone dreams.'

On 1 December, the Japanese Navy unexpectedly changed all its call-signs. This usually happened every six months; the last call-sign change had been on 1 November. Something was afoot, but Lieutenant Commander Joseph J. Rochefort, head of the Radio Unit of the 14th Naval District in Hawaii, had to admit to his boss, the commander-in-chief of the Pacific Fleet, Admiral Husband E. Kimmel, that he still did not know where the Japanese aircraft carriers were. The consensus was that they were still in home waters.

American efforts were hampered by a large amount of dummy traffic and transmissions sent to multiple addressees. However, Rochefort quickly noticed that no communications were coming from the carriers or submarines. The other traffic, however, seemed to indicate an attack to the south on Siam (Thailand) or Singapore.

Also on 1 December, a Purple message from Tokyo to Washington reminded staff how to destroy their codes. Instructions on how to destroy their Purple machines had been given five days earlier. Another message that day implied that the Japanese were planning to attack British and Dutch possessions in Southeast Asia, not the US. It said that the code machines in London, Singapore and Manila had been disposed of, while the one in Batavia (Jakarta) had been returned to Japan.

The strike force now at sea picked up a blanket broadcast to all ships which said: 'NIITAKA-YAMA NOBORE – climb Mount Niitaka.' It was the code to proceed with the attack.

Back in Honolulu, a turf war had broken out over wire taps with the FBI, causing the Navy to cut theirs on the lines to the Japanese Consulate, but not before they had overheard the instruction to burn all codebooks and secret documents. The following day, 3 December, a Purple message from Tokyo was deciphered telling the Washington embassy to do the same. Reading the Magic decrypt, President Roosevelt concluded that war was imminent and inevitable. The only question was where the attack would come.

Along with the codebooks and secret documents, the Washington, D.C., embassy was told to destroy all but one of its Purple machines. First, they had to be dismantled with a screwdriver. The parts then had to be hammered flat and dissolved in acid supplied by the naval attaché. In Tokyo, too, the US military attaché was told to destroy war department documents.

On 4 December, monitoring stations picked up a weather forecast saying, 'north wind cloudy'. However, the second mention said, confusingly: 'North wind clear, may become slightly cloudy'. While American intelligence officers were relieved that there was no mention of 'east wind rain', they also concluded that this was not a genuine warning that Japanese–Soviet relations had broken down.

Following Hull's rejection of the Japanese ultimatum, representatives of the Imperial Army and Navy met the Foreign Minister in Tokyo on 5 December to discuss what time they should send a detailed notification to the US that amounted to the declaration of war. It was decided that the planned delivery should be postponed half an hour, until 1 pm EST on 7 December, an hour after dawn in Hawaii. Vice Admiral Seiichi Itō asked Foreign Minister Shigenori Tōgō not to 'cable the notification to the embassy in Washington too early'.

Around 1 pm on 6 December, Japan's declaration of war arrived in the cable room of the Foreign Ministry. The 5,000-word notification was broken down into 14 parts for ease of transmission. These then got enciphered on the Purple machines. A shorter note warned the Washington, D.C., embassy that a reply to Hull's note was on its way. This had been intercepted and deciphered before the Japanese had begun sending the first 13 parts of the notification. The crucial fourteenth part was to be held back until the last moment.

The first 13 parts of notification were intercepted and US Army and Navy codebreakers got to work. By then, the cipher clerks in the Japanese embassy were working on the notification too. Americans had finished deciphering all 13 parts when the Japanese took a break after deciphering the first seven or eight parts for a leaving party at the Mayflower Hotel. Meanwhile, cryptographers in the State Department were encoding a personal appeal for peace from the President of the United States to the Emperor of Japan.

In Honolulu, army counterintelligence was concerned over a tapped phone call between a Japanese journalist and her editor in Tokyo in which she said, 'the hibiscus and poinsettia are in bloom'. Surely this was code. At the same time, Takeo Yoshikawa was using the cable company RCA to telegraph home details of the shipping in Pearl Harbor.

In Washington, D.C., the first 13 parts of the notification were being circulated as Magic. When Roosevelt read it, he said simply: 'This means war.' With him was aide Harry Hopkins, who advised Roosevelt to strike the first blow.

'We can't do that,' said Roosevelt. 'We are a democracy and peaceful people.'

Others privy to Magic that night agreed that negotiations were at an end. Everyone was on tenterhooks while awaiting the 14th and final part. Checks were made to see whether one of the monitoring stations had picked it up but had neglected to forward it. In fact, the Japanese Foreign Office in Tokyo was holding it up until the last possible moment.

Finally, 14 hours after the end of the last transmission, the 14th part was intercepted. It took an hour for the Americans to decipher it. Like the rest of the notification it was in English. In the meantime, another message was picked up. This one was in Japanese and had to be sent to the Signal Intelligence Service for translation. Nevertheless, the Americans were way ahead of the cipher clerks in the Japanese embassy, who had been stood down for the night and were recalled again at 8 am.

The 14th part had been deciphered by the Americans by 4 am. It was rushed to the White House and the State Department. By 9 am, the second message had been translated. It instructed the Japanese embassy to deliver the 14-part notification to Secretary Hull at 1 pm. This sent the cipher clerks in the Japanese embassy into a frenzy. They had the rest of the notification to decipher and only one Purple machine to do it on.

While the first wave of Japanese planes took off from the carriers, Ambassador Nomura called Hull to request a meeting at 1 pm. Another Japanese message had been intercepted, this one in plain language, and ordered the destruction of the last Purple machine in the Washington, D.C., embassy.

Chief of Staff George C. Marshall sent out an enciphered warning to his commanding generals in Hawaii, the Caribbean, along the West Coast and in the Philippines – but the despatch to the Philippines was to be given priority as it was thought to be the most likely candidate for an attack.

Around 12.30 pm, the Japanese embassy staff had finished deciphering part 14 of the notification. But the previous 13 parts were still being typed up. The embassy then called the State Department, requesting that Nomura's meeting with Hull be postponed until 1.45 pm.

Within minutes of the call, Japanese bombers and torpedo planes were attacking the US Pacific Fleet in Pearl Harbor. By the time Nomura arrived at the State Department with the notification at 2.05 pm, Hull had received a call from Roosevelt, saying he had an unconfirmed report that Pearl Harbor was under attack.

When the Japanese ambassador turned up at the State Department, Hull kept them waiting. At 2.20 pm, he invited Nomura into his office. He did not ask him to sit down. Nomura told Hull that his government had instructed him to deliver this document to him at 1 pm, but it was delayed because of the difficulty in decoding it.

In his memoirs, Hull recalled: 'I made a pretense of glancing through the note. I knew its contents already but naturally could give no indication of the fact … When I finished skimming the pages, I turned to Nomura and put my eye on him.

"'I must say," I said, "that in all my conversations with you during the last nine months I have never uttered one word of untruth. This is borne out absolutely by the record. In all my fifty years of public service I have never seen a document that was more crowded with infamous falsehoods and distortions – infamous falsehoods and distortion on a scale so huge that I never imagined until today that any government on his planet was capable of uttering them.'"

For the moment, it seemed that the Japanese attempt to maintain the element of surprise had paid off. However, their failure to open hostilities without first declaring war would be part of the charges laid against Japanese war leaders when they were tried and convicted in the Tokyo War Crimes Trial after the war. Some of them paid with their lives.

The USS West Virginia *after the attack.*

Marshall's warning arrived in Hawaii after the attack had begun. It then had to be deciphered and only reached the commanding general, Major General Walter Short, at 3 pm. After a quick glance, he threw it straight in the bin.

Already, monitoring stations had picked up a Japanese news broadcast announcing the 'death-defying raid' on Pearl Harbor. It broke off to give a weather forecast: 'West wind clear.'

Less than eight hours later, the Japanese attacked the British colony of Hong Kong. There were landings on Malaya and the Philippines, and attacks on Guam, Wake and Singapore. Both Roosevelt and Churchill knew that the Japanese were going to attack, they just did not know where. The answer was – not just Pearl Harbor, but across the east Pacific and Southeast Asia.

FLIGHT OF THE NAZIS – DID HITLER SURVIVE?

After it became clear that Germany was going to lose the war, escape routes were set up to smuggle senior Nazis and war criminals to safety. These were known as ratlines. These were sometimes organized by *Werwolf*, an organization dedicated to continuing a guerrilla war against the occupying forces, or fanatical Nazis who aimed to create a Fourth Reich, a successor to Hitler's Third Reich.

Hitler, we now know, committed suicide in his bunker in Berlin. But that was not clear at the time. His body had been burned in the gardens of the Reich Chancellery, which had then been occupied by the Red Army. The charred remains were taken by the Soviets, who spirited them away. This led to the belief that he might have escaped and found sanctuary in South America.

The easiest way out of war-torn Europe was via Spain, whose dictator General Francisco Franco had been sympathetic to the Fascist and Nazi causes. In 1945, Europe was awash with some 40 million displaced persons and prisoners of war, many of whom had no papers. Nazi war criminals could surrender under false names or disappear into the crowds that flooded the roads. To escape, what they needed were false identity papers, which were often arranged by the Vatican.

As early as 1942, when the war was already going badly for Italy, representatives of the Catholic Church made contact with Argentina to enquire whether Catholic immigrants might be welcome there. One should remember that Hitler was a Catholic. Argentina had a substantial German population and its democratically elected government was toppled by a military coup in 1943, aided by Colonel Juan Perón, who later became president. Although the US forced Argentina to declare war on the Axis powers a month before the end of the war, the country was happy to welcome former fascists to emigrate there.

After the end of the war, the Austrian Catholic bishop Alois Hudal, a Nazi sympathizer, became active in ministering to German-speaking prisoners of war and internees then held in camps throughout Italy. He helped a number of wanted Nazi war criminals escape, including the commander of the Sobibor and Treblinka death camps, Franz Stangl. Using a Red Cross passport, Stangl escaped to Syria. Nazi hunter Simon Wiesenthal eventually tracked him to Brazil. In 1967, he was extradited to West Germany, where he admitted killing around one million people. 'My conscience is clear. I was simply doing my duty', he said. Sentenced to life imprisonment, he died in jail in 1971.

False papers were provided by the Vatican and the International Committee of the Red Cross, which escapees could then use to get visas. The ICRC was supposed to do background checks, but usually the word of a bishop was enough.

Another war criminal aided by Hudal was Adolf Eichmann, who had organized the Holocaust. He had managed to hide out in a little village in Lower Saxony until 1950, when Hudal's organization provided him with false papers to emigrate to Argentina. In 1960, he was kidnapped by Mossad, Israel's intelligence agency, and taken to Israel where he was put on trial. He showed no remorse – insisting, of course, that he was only obeying orders.

In his plea for a pardon, he said: 'There is a need to draw a line between the leaders responsible and the people like me forced to serve as mere instruments in the hands of the leaders. I was not a responsible leader, and as such do not feel myself guilty.'

Nevertheless, he was convicted of war crimes and hanged in 1962.

Alois Hudal, who smuggled Nazi war criminals out of Europe after the end of the war.

Others fared better. Eichmann's right-hand man, Alois Brunner, who deported Jews to the death camps from Austria, Greece, Slovakia, Macedonia and France, was helped by Hubal and others to get out of West Germany in 1954 on a fake Red Cross passport, first to Rome, then to Egypt, where he worked as a weapons dealer. He moved on to Syria, where he worked for the Ministry of the Interior, along with another Nazi, advising on torture and repression.

Requests for his extradition were refused. In 1954, he was tried *in absentia* in France and given two death sentences. In an interview with a reporter from the *Chicago Sun-Times* he was unrepentant. 'The Jews deserved to die,' he said. 'I have no regrets. If I had the chance, I would do it again … All of them deserved to die because they were the Devil's agents and human garbage.'

He lost an eye and fingers from his left hand due to letter bombs. Further attempts to extradite him also failed. In his final years, he was held under house arrest in a basement in Damascus. He died there in 2001.

Although he helped war criminals escape justice, Hudal was also unapologetic. Indeed, he thanked God for allowing him to help these men. The war, he thought, was simply about economic rivalry. That was 'why I felt duty bound after 1945 to devote my whole charitable work mainly to former National Socialists and Fascists, especially to so-called "war criminals".' He considered them victims. Until his death in 1963, he continued trying to arrange amnesties for former Nazis.

Another ratline was run through Rome by a network of Croatian priests, members of the Franciscan order, led by Father Krunoslav Draganović and with its headquarters at the San Girolamo degli Illirici Seminary College. He had been a member of the Ustaše, the Croatian fascist group who murdered hundreds of thousands of Serbs, Jews, Roma and Croatian political dissidents as well as the king of Yugoslavia, Alexander I. With the help of the Italians, Ante Pavelić became dictator of the Independent State of Croatia from 1941.

Disguised as a priest, he entered Italy with a Peruvian passport in 1946 and was given sanctuary in a number of properties that belonged to the Vatican, including a monastery near the papal summer residence of Castel Gandolfo.

In 1948, he met Draganović, who helped him get a Red Cross passport in the Hungarian name of Pál Aranyos. He then fled to Argentina, where he became a security advisor to Argentinian president Juan Perón. In 1950, Pavelić was given amnesty and allowed to stay in Argentina along with 34,000 other Croats, including former Nazi collaborators. Through contacts with Evita Perón, he became the owner of a building company.

He survived several assassination attempts organized by a Serbian former Royal Yugoslav Army officer, though a bullet lodged in his spine. When Perón fell from power, the new government granted an extradition request from Yugoslavia. So Pavelić moved to Chile, then sought asylum in Spain, where he died in 1959.

Other former Ustaše members and Nazi refugees hiding in Austria were helped to cross the border into Italy. There, they were given sanctuary, often in Draganović's Franciscan monastery, while documentation was arranged. Then they were given passage on ships out of Genoa bound for South America.

The Vatican knew what was going on. The US Counter Intelligence Corps said that some wanted Croats were given sanctuary in the Vatican itself. Otherwise they were seen travelling between the Vatican and the Monastery of San Girolamo degli Illirici in a car with Vatican plates, which could not be stopped because it had diplomatic immunity.

The Americans did not do anything about it. They used Draganović's ratline themselves, to smuggle key scientists and important military strategists out of Europe who were also wanted by the Soviets.

One of the biggest names to escape was Dr Josef Mengele, who had conducted experiments on live prisoners in Auschwitz. Taken as a prisoner of war by the Americans, he escaped detection as he did not have the usual SS blood group tattoo on his arm. Assisted by a network of former SS members, he used the ratline to travel to Genoa, where he obtained a passport from the International Committee of the Red Cross under the alias 'Helmut Gregor', and sailed to Argentina in 1949.

When extradition proceedings began in 1959, he fled to Paraguay. With the West German government and Mossad on his tail, he moved on to Brazil where he drowned in 1979 after having a stroke while swimming. He was buried under the name Wolfgang Gerhard, one of his many aliases. His body was exhumed in 1985 and identified as Mengele by his son. This was confirmed by DNA testing in 1992.

While Perón was still in power, Argentina sent diplomats and intelligence agents to encourage Nazi and fascist war criminals to come and make their home in Argentina, establishing their own ratlines. An immigration commission was set up to arrange Argentine citizenship and employment. Catholic bishops were also sent to encourage French collaborators to come too.

One such was Émile Dewoite, a French industrialist who made planes for the Luftwaffe. Charged with collaboration, he fled to Spain after the liberation, then went to Argentina. In 1948 he was tried *in absentia* in France and sentenced to 20 years' hard labour.

According to Nazi hunter Simon Wiesenthal, former SS men had set up the ODESSA operation to help veterans escape, though later researchers doubt that a single organization of this name actually existed. However, it is clear that former SS men did operate ratlines.

Other ratlines were run by a network of right-wing extremists in Finland, originally set up for use in the expected Soviet occupation. They ran safe houses and a small fishing company that ferried Nazis and refugees to Sweden.

In June 1946, the US occupation force set up the Gehlen Organization under former German intelligence officer Richard Gehlen. It employed former military officers of the *Wehrmacht* as well as former intelligence officers of the SS and the SD experienced in spying on the Soviet Union. It cooperated closely with the CIA when it was formed in 1947 and was superseded by West Germany's Federal Intelligence Service, the BND, in 1956. Alois Brunner was thought to be a member before he escaped in 1954.

SS man Otto Skorzeny, who famously rescued Mussolini after he'd fallen from power, was interned after the war. He was charged with violating the laws of war for wearing an American uniform behind Allied lines during the Battle of the Bulge. On the run, he contacted Richard Gehlen and was recruited for the Gehlen Organization. With the help of Gehlen he set up *Die Spinne* – The Spider – another organization that helped as many as 600 former SS men escape to Spain and Argentina.

When his photograph taken in a café on the Champs Elysées appeared in the press in 1950, he went on the run again, until the Spanish provided the papers he needed to move to Madrid. He and other former Nazis went on to train the Egyptian Army and he became an advisor to Juan Perón. Although he still harboured ambitions to start a Fourth Reich, he was declared 'denazified' by a West German government arbitration board. In the 1960s he was involved in neo-Nazi activities in Spain. He died in Madrid in 1975, aged 67. His ashes were interred at his family plot in Vienna. His funerals in Madrid and Vienna were attended by former SS colleagues who gave the Hitler salute and sang some of Hitler's favourite songs.

The 'Butcher of Lyon' Klaus Barbie, Gestapo chief in the city, worked for America's Counter Intelligence Corp, who helped him escape to Bolivia in 1951, again with the help of Krunoslav Draganović. There he worked for the BND. He went on to work for the military junta in Peru. He was arrested in La Paz in 1983 and extradited to France, where he was jailed. He died in prison in 1991, aged 77.

In the late 1940s and early 1950s, some thought that Hitler had not committed suicide in Berlin, but had escaped to Argentina via Spain. The theory is that he left the *Führerbunker* and made his way via a series of underground tunnels to Tempelhof airfield. Hitler's personal belongings were seen being put on board planes carrying escaping Nazis on 21 April 1945, the day after he made his last public appearance. A compound was later found at Misiones, deep inside the Argentine jungle, that was filled with Nazi memorabilia.

In November 1945, a heavily redacted FBI report said Hitler was hiding out in the foothills of the southern Andes after he and his party was landed in the Gulf of Matías, Patagonia, by two submarines two and a half weeks after the fall of Berlin. Six Argentine officials were there to greet him. He had shaved off his distinctive moustache. Pack horses were loaded with supplies to make the trip inland to stay with German families in the towns of San Antonio, Viedma, Neuquen, Musters, Carmena and Rason.

A CIA document from 1955 contained a photocopy of a photograph of a man calling himself Phillip Citroen, said to be a former SS trooper, taken in Tunja, Colombia, in 1954. Alongside him was another man purporting to be Adolf Schuttlemayer. Citroen insisted that Schuttlemayer was Hitler and that he left Colombia for Argentina around 1955.

A US Secret Service mock-up of Hitler in disguise.

Citroen commented that, since ten years had passed since the end of the war, the Allies could no longer prosecute Hitler as a war criminal, though it is hard to imagine that the statute of limitations anywhere in the world would apply to mass murder. Indeed, Nazi concentration camp guards are being convicted to this day. However, the figure in the photograph was so confident that he had even grown his famous moustache back.

A subsequent CIA investigation found that Hitler's alleged presence in Colombia was an open secret in some circles. In a country 'overly populated with former German Nazis', Citroen told an agency source, Schuttlemayer was idolized by those who knew his real identity. They called him '*Der Führer*' and honoured him with the old Nazi salute.

The CIA chief in Caracas was sceptical but continued to pursue the case. He was eventually told by his superiors that 'enormous efforts could be expended on this matter with remote possibilities of establishing anything concrete'. So Schuttlemayer, whoever he was, was thereafter left alone and, in 1956, the West German government issued a death certificate for Adolf Hitler.

In 2017, a team of French researchers persuaded the Russian government to let them inspect the last two pieces of Hitler known to exist: a bullet-shot chunk of skull and a set of teeth. DNA testing showed that the skull fragment belonged to a woman. But Hitler's teeth were then identified by his personal dentist and his assistant, and by an X-ray taken in 1944.

'There is no possible doubt. Our study proves that Hitler died in 1945,' the French pathologist Philippe Charlier told Agence France-Presse after his paper was published in the *European Journal of Internal Medicine*. 'He did not flee to Argentina in a submarine. He is not in a hidden base in Antarctica or on the dark side of the moon.'

One of the reasons that conspiracy theories about the fate of Hitler abounded was that lies were told about his death from the beginning. On the day after Hitler's suicide it was announced that he had died a few hours earlier, fighting at the head of his troops. A doctor even testified in a deposition that he had tried to save the wounded leader.

'A shell fragment had pierced the uniform, went through his chest and entered the lungs on both sides,' he told a court. 'It was no use to do anything.'

In his will, Hitler specified that his body be destroyed. He did not want to be hung up from a lamppost as Mussolini had been. When the Red Army found the charred remains of his body buried in a shell hole, the Soviets conducted a post-mortem and concluded that he had committed suicide.

However, in the Cold War, it suited the Soviets to keep the West guessing. At a press conference, Marshal Georgi Zhukov, who had accepted the German surrender after the Battle of Berlin, on the orders of Soviet leader Joseph Stalin announced that Hitler had not committed suicide. When asked at the Potsdam Conference in July 1945 how Hitler had died, Stalin said he was living either 'in Spain or Argentina'.

In July 1945, British newspapers repeated comments from a Soviet officer that a charred body discovered by the Soviets was 'a very poor double'. American newspapers also repeated dubious quotes, such as that of the Russian garrison commandant of Berlin, who claimed that Hitler had 'gone into hiding somewhere in Europe'. In June 1945, 68 per cent of Americans polled thought Hitler was still alive. Weird and wonderful tales of where Hitler had ended up proliferated.

The Soviet Union retained Hitler's body for decades until, in the 1970s, the KGB was finally told to destroy the corpse, leaving only a shard of the skull and the jawbone in the Kremlin's possession.

The strategy worked. There was mass public confusion about when, how and whether Hitler had died. In an information vacuum, newspapers quickly filled up with stories of sketchy sightings of the Nazi leader. Hitler was seen as a croupier in a casino in France. He was a shepherd in the Alps, a hermit in a cave. So widespread was the disinformation that even General Dwight D. Eisenhower entertained the possibility of Hitler's survival.

In 2013, the *Daily Mail* recounted the story of Hitler's escape from the ruins of Berlin. It began with the besieged leader contemplating his future while staring at a portrait of Frederick the Great, his lifelong hero.

'A Fourth Reich would surely rise, and he would be needed to lead it,' the *Mail* imagined Hitler thinking. 'That left one option: escape.'

So, three days before his supposed suicide, Hitler ordered two corpses to be dressed as himself and Eva Braun, who he married hours before their deaths. He waited until the stroke of midnight, then slipped out of his bunker via a secret tunnel and sneaked through the bombed-out city. He rendezvoused with an aeroplane he had arranged to meet him on an abandoned thoroughfare, then flew to Denmark and then Spain, where a commandeered submarine took him to South America, landing at the small port of Necochea, some 483 km (300 miles) south of Buenos Aires. After 17 years in hiding, he died on 13 February 1962, aged 73.

'To most of us, such a story sounds like utter fantasy,' the *Mail* noted at the end of this adventure. 'But there are some who regard it as the absolute truth.'

After all, a U-boat did disappear after the end of the war and many top Nazis did end up in South America.

SALON KITTY

Hitler had dodged several assassination attempts throughout his political career and was always conscious of conspiracies against him. To root them out, he used spymaster Walter Schellenberg and his boss Reinhard Heydrich. The two of them had a complex relationship. While Heydrich was flagrantly unfaithful to his wife, Lina, with numerous mistresses and prostitutes, Schellenberg became her discreet lover.

Even so, they would spend domestic evenings playing bridge, or Schellenberg and Heydrich would go out on the town together. Heydrich was already a patron of the Pension Kitty, a high-class brothel run by Kitty Schmidt, who kept four or five prostitutes on the premises. Clients could also select a partner from photographic albums who would then be brought by taxi.

In 1939, Heydrich was charged with investigating the source of a high-level leak that threatened to give the Allies advanced warning of Germany's plan to attack through the Ardennes to take France and the Low Countries. If the enemy got wind of this and strengthened the defences at this weak point it could have proved disastrous to the invasion.

One evening while out with Schellenberg, Heydrich came up with the idea of infiltrating a brothel patronized by officers, government officials and other high-flyers, where alcohol and pretty women might loosen an informer's tongue. It was essentially a conspiracy against their own comrades and allies.

Reinhard Heydrich, the brains behind Salon Kitty.

Schellenberg was assigned to the operation. The problem was the SS had little experience of running brothels. But Kitty Schmidt, madam of Pension Kitty, did. A former prostitute, she had opened her first brothel in 1922. On the advice of wealthy clients, she banked her profits in London, escaping the worst of hyperinflation under the Weimar Republic.

When Hitler came to power in 1933, business continued as usual, though several Jewish friends left for London, where they managed her financial affairs for her. By 1937, the Nazi authorities cracked down on money being transferred out of the country and Kitty sent girls to London with cash sewn into their corsets. Influential clients warned her that war was coming and, in March 1939, she decided to flee the country. But she was arrested at the Dutch border and ended up in Schellenberg's office.

He knew what she had been up to and gave her a choice. Either she could work for him or go to a concentration camp. On 27 July 1939 – five weeks before war broke out – Schellenberg took over Pension Kitty and transformed it into Berlin's most notorious brothel: Salon Kitty. The place was closed down for ten days, ostensibly for renovation, while microphones were concealed in the walls. A listening station was installed in the basement, with recording equipment using wax discs.

The brothel needed to be staffed. A top-secret memo was sent out requesting 'Women and girls, who are intelligent, multilingual, nationalistically minded and furthermore man-crazy.'

When this proved unproductive, Schellenberg contacted the chief of police, a former head of the vice squad who knew a large number of working girls. The selection board consisted of a psychologist, doctors and linguists. The women had to be between the ages of 20 and 30, single, with few family ties and loyal to National Socialism.

The recruits were inducted into the SS and swore a vow of secrecy along with an oath of allegiance to Hitler. Training included basic espionage skills and languages, along with indoctrination in Nazi ideology. They were not told that the bedrooms in the brothel were bugged. Instead, they would have to produce a written report after every encounter. These would be checked against transcripts from the recordings.

Salon Kitty was well supplied with food and liquor, despite wartime shortages, and word of its existence was circulated in diplomatic and other official circles. Special customers sent by the *SS* were given a password. If a client said 'I come from Rothenburg', they were shown the albums containing pictures of the most attractive girls.

In early April 1940, Operation Salon Kitty had its first success. *Obersturmführer* Wolfgang Reichert, who had distinguished himself in Poland with the *Waffen SS*, let slip that he was being posted to Flensburg on the Danish border. On 9 April, Germany invaded Denmark and Norway.

Soon after, Count Gian Galeazzo Ciano, Italy's foreign minister and the son-in-law of Mussolini, visited Salon Kitty and was recorded criticizing Hitler. On 20 April – Hitler's birthday – Schellenberg was promoted *Sturmbannführer* and the operation was expanded, with two dozen *SS* men listening in around the clock. However, Heydrich still patronized Kitty's and found that he had been overheard and recorded. He ordered Schellenberg to move the listening post to the *SD* headquarters in Prinz Albrechtstrasse, where his office was.

The sitting room of Salon Kitty, where conversations were overheard.

Another visitor to Salon Kitty was British agent Roger Wilson. He had infiltrated Nazi Germany as the deputy press attaché in the Romanian embassy, calling himself Ljubo Kolchev – a name of a Romanian refugee exiled in London.

His suspicions were soon aroused when he noticed that all the girls were accomplished linguists and well versed in current affairs. He also noticed that new cables were being laid in the street outside, as the listening post in the basement was being moved on Heydrich's orders. Wilson reported his suspicions to London and was told to continue his investigation.

He then noticed that, in the rooms in Salon Kitty, there were depressions high up in the wallpaper, which, he suspected, hid microphones. And the new cables he had seen being laid in the street outside, he concluded, connected the microphones to an external listening post. London then sent technicians who, under cover of darkness, managed to tap a couple of the circuits. This allowed the British to set up a listening post of their own.

Hitler's propaganda minister Joseph Goebbels and Joseph 'Sepp' Dietrich, the highest-ranking officer in the *Waffen-SS*, also visited Salon Kitty, but gave little away.

Spanish Foreign Minister Ramón Serrano Suñer, who was also dictator General Francisco Franco's brother-in-law, was taken to Salon Kitty by the German foreign minister, Joachim von Ribbentrop. Over a drink in the salon, they discussed plans to take Gibraltar from the British, giving the Axis domination over the Mediterranean and Britain's western approaches.

When a Japanese diplomat in Berlin to conclude the German-Italian-Japanese Tripartite Pact visited Salon Kitty, Frau Schmidt feared that she might fall foul of the Nazi racial purity laws, but she got permission for him to pick one of the Rothenburg girls.

In February 1941, an Italian embassy official told one of the girls that he feared the war would ruin Italy. The Italians were suffering reverses in North Africa and, in March, Hitler sent the *Afrika Korps*. The Italian invasion of Greece was also going badly and Germany had to go to the Italians' assistance, delaying Hitler's planned attack on Russia. However, Schellenberg ensured that diplomats from neither the Soviet Union nor the

United States patronized Salon Kitty. Both nations were about to become enemies and he feared that the operation might have been compromised.

After Germany's attack on the Soviet Union in June 1941, more indiscretions poured in. Schellenberg was promoted to *SS-Standartenführer*, or full colonel, and made head of Department VI, the *SD* foreign intelligence service. He celebrated by paying a visit to Salon Kitty himself. This time, the recording equipment was turned off.

Romania signed the Tripartite Pact in November 1941, putting Ronald Wilson in danger. Then the *SS* discovered that the real Ljubo Kolchev was in London. Wilson was arrested, tortured and sent to Sachsenhausen concentration camp.

On 17 July 1942, a bomb hit the building, destroying the top floors and putting Salon Kitty out of commission. The microphones were quickly removed. Two days later, Salon Kitty re-opened, but activities were confined to the ground floor and the *SD* had to depend only on the written reports submitted by the girls.

With the war turning against Germany, Salon Kitty's clientele were largely men returning from the front. Ribbentrop and Wilhelm Canaris, head of the *Abwehr*, discovered that the *SD* had been bugging the brothel and told men from their ministries to avoid the place. As discipline slackened, the girls began to have all-night parties and their reports became increasingly unreliable.

As Salon Kitty was no longer a valuable intelligence asset, Schellenberg decided to close down the operation and concentrate on other things – including making peace overtures to the Allies on behalf of Himmler.

When Berlin fell, the Soviets tried to use Salon Kitty to their own advantage. So did the British and Americans when it fell into their zone of occupation. In the midst of these rival interests, Kitty Schmidt kept her own counsel, dying at the age of 71 in 1954. It was later revealed that another establishment along the lines of Salon Kitty had been run by the Gestapo in Vienna.

A ROYAL CONSPIRACY

Hitler was loath to go to war with Britain. He saw the British as Germanic–Aryan people and admired the British Empire. He wanted his own empire on Continental Europe, while Britain could keep its empire overseas. And he had a plan.

He knew that many of the British aristocracy were sympathetic to his cause. They saw Nazi Germany as a bulwark against Russian Communism. But he thought he could go one better. For centuries, the British royal family and the royal families of the German states had intermarried. The British royal family was German, after all.

His proposal was that David, the Prince of Wales who went on to become Edward VIII in 1936, should marry a German princess. Indeed, there was talk of his marriage to Princess Karoline Mathilde of Schleswig-Holstein-Sonderburg-Glücksburg before World War I, but she had married Count Hans of Solms-Baruth in 1920. David (hereafter Edward), though, was still single.

For Hitler, the most promising candidate was Princess Friederike, the daughter of Duke Ernst August III of Brunswick and Duchess Viktoria Luise, the only daughter of Kaiser Wilhelm II. Her father was a prominent donor to the Nazi Party and often wore the brown uniform of a Storm Trooper, while her brother was in the SS. Friederike herself was a member of the *Bund Deutscher Mädel* – the League of German Girls, the female branch of the Hitler Youth. However, her parents were not keen as Edward was 22 years older than their 17-year-old daughter. Before World War I, the duchess herself, just two years older than the prince, had been a candidate for his hand.

At the 1936 Berlin Olympics, Friederike met Prince Paul, the crown prince of Greece and first cousin of the future Duke of Edinburgh. They married two years later though he was 16 years her senior. By then, Edward was already deeply involved with Wallis Simpson.

The Prince of Wales favoured Americans and courted married women in the hope that he would not become too involved with them. Although his father, George V, has let it be known that his children would be permitted to marry commoners, it was still rather expected that the heir to the throne should marry European royalty.

However, there were problems and none of his affairs seemed to last long. Lady Thelma Furness, the daughter of an American diplomat, may have put her finger on it. After she had dumped him for Prince Aly Khan, racehorse owner and head of the Ismaili Muslims, she openly complained of Edward's poor sexual performance. It seems that he was not very well endowed and she scandalized society by calling him 'the little man'. At Osborne Naval College, where the teenage prince trained to be an officer, the other cadets joked that he should be called 'Sardines' rather than 'Whales'.

At Burrough Court, the country seat of Viscount and Lady Furness, he was introduced to fellow guests Wallis Simpson and her husband Ernest. Wallis had been born in Baltimore. Her first husband, navy flier Lieutenant Earl Winfield 'Win' Spencer, had been an alcoholic and a sadist who had numerous extra-marital affairs with both men and women. Wallis, for her part, launched herself on the diplomatic scene in Washington, D.C., bedding the Italian ambassador and a senior Argentine diplomat.

In a belated honeymoon, Win took her on a trip to the Far East, where they visited the brothels of Shanghai and Hong Kong. There, she was said to have learned the ancient erotic arts of Fang Chung which, it was claimed, could arouse even the most passionless of men.

Win eventually decided that he was gay and moved in with a handsome young artist. This left Wallis free to take on a string of lovers, including

Edward, Prince of Wales in 1919, later King Edward VIII.

the Italian naval attaché Count Galeazzo Ciano, who would become Italy's foreign minister after marrying Mussolini's daughter.

Wallis met her second husband, shipbroker Ernest Simpson, in New York. American-born, he naturalized as a British subject when he joined the Coldstream Guards during World War I. Like Wallis, he was married, but the couple quickly divorced their respective partners, married and moved to London.

After Wallis was introduced to the Prince of Wales by Lady Furness, the two of them would often make up a foursome with Wallis' husband and his mistress, Mary Raffray. In 1934, the prince holidayed with Mrs Simpson at Biarritz. The following year, they were photographed leaving a lingerie shop in Kitzbühel, where they were having a skiing holiday together. In May, the gossip came home to London when the prince danced with Mrs Simpson at his parents' Silver Jubilee ball.

Powerful press barons kept these stories out of the British newspapers, but they were widely published abroad, which presented Hitler with another opportunity. He already knew of the Simpsons' political leanings as Sir Oswald Mosley, leader of the British Union of Fascists, was a frequent visitor at the Simpsons' London apartment in Bryanston Court, Marylebone. Mosley used the prince's name when canvassing for financial support among the upper classes and, in the summer of 1935, his fascist-leaning January Club was renamed the Windsor Club.

Living in the same block as the Simpsons was Stephanie Julianne von Hohenlohe. An Austrian princess, she was a close confidante of Hitler and operated as a German spy in Britain and America. A lover of Viscount Rothermere, owner of the *Daily Mail*, she encouraged the newspaper's pre-war pro-Nazi stance.

Both the king and the prime minister were growing concerned about the prince's inappropriate affair and called in Scotland Yard. Superintendent Albert Canning, a veteran of Special Branch, quickly discovered that Wallis was two-timing the prince with a car salesman named Guy Marcus Trundle. MI5 was also on the case. With Stephanie Julianne von Hohenlohe living there, MI5 was concerned that Bryanston Court was a nest of Nazi spies – one of them Wallis Simpson herself.

Princess Stephanie moved in the same circles as the Prince of Wales and Wallis Simpson, where she peddled the Nazi line. Her principal target was the prince, as Hitler wanted a pro-German king on the throne – even better if he had a pro-Nazi consort by his side.

Lady Emerald Cunard was also one of Princess Stephanie's key patrons. She regularly invited the Prince of Wales and Wallis Simpson to dinner. Nancy Astor condemned her for encouraging the pro-Nazi leanings of the Prince of Wales, though Lady Astor was an admirer of Hitler herself.

Hitler then sent Joachim von Ribbentrop to join the fray, as ambassador to the Court of St James's. At a dinner hosted by Lady Cunard, the American society diarist and MP Sir Henry 'Chips' Channon noted: 'Much gossip about the Prince of Wales' alleged Nazi leanings; he is alleged to have been influenced by Emerald Cunard who is rather *eprise* [in love with] Herr Ribbentrop through Mrs Simpson.'

When the Prince of Wales and Ribbentrop met at a dinner party, they got on rather well, especially as the prince spoke German fluently, having visited his family there often. 'After all he is half German,' Ribbentrop telegrammed Hitler.

Ribbentrop, as it turned out, was only half right. 'Every drop of blood in my veins is German,' the prince told Diana Mitford, wife of Oswald Mosley and a friend of Hitler. During the Depression, unemployment and poor housing had been causes close to the prince's heart and he thought that National Socialism had done much to solve these problems in Germany.

France, he thought, was weak and degenerate, and the Soviets had executed his godfather Tsar Nicholas II and his family. The danger – especially for the royals – came from the Communists. War between Britain and Germany, he believed, would hand a victory to the Russians. 'I hope and believe we shall never fight a war again,' he told the Austrian ambassador, 'but if so we must be on the winning side, and that will be German, not the French.'

Chips Channon had his suspicions. The prince was going 'the dictator way and is pro-German,' he said. 'I shouldn't be surprised if he aimed at making himself a mild dictator – a difficult enough task for an English king.'

Soon, Ribbentrop began sending Wallis 17 carnations every day. The prince's cousin the Duke of Württemberg said that 17 was the number of times Wallis and Ribbentrop had slept together. He also said that the prince was impotent and only the oriental arts practised by Mrs Simpson could satisfy him.

Spymaster and diplomat R. H. Bruce Lockhart arranged a meeting between the prince and the Kaiser's grandson, Prince Louis Ferdinand, noting afterwards: 'The Prince of Wales was quite pro-Hitler and said it was no business of ours to interfere in Germany's internal affairs either re Jews or re anything else and added that dictators are very popular these days and that we might want one in England before long.'

At Ribbentrop's suggestion, the prince set up exchange visits for British and German veterans of World War I and got a dressing down by the king for interfering in foreign policy. Nevertheless, he supported the Italian invasion of Abyssinia (now Ethiopia) on the grounds that fascist efficiency would improve its medieval economy.

At the funeral of George V, the new king's cousin, Carl Eduard, Duke of Saxe-Coburg and Gotha, marched behind the coffin in full Nazi uniform. A childhood friend of Edward VIII, Carl Eduard was president of the Anglo-German Fellowship, which was decidedly pro-Nazi. When Carl Eduard broached the subject of talks between Hitler and Prime Minister Stanley Baldwin, Edward said: 'Who is king here? Baldwin or I? I myself wish to talk to Hitler and will do so here or in Germany.'

At Fort Belvedere, Edward VIII's country house, government boxes went missing and top-secret papers were left around for Wallis to read. The secret codes used by British embassies were compromised. Edward discussed everything with Mrs Simpson and showed her state papers. This was clearly a security risk. According to under-secretary of state for foreign affairs Lord Vansittart, she was 'in the pocket of Ribbentrop'. Vansittart's junior in the Foreign Office, Ralph Wigram, had earlier written a top-secret memo saying that 'Mrs S is very close to Hoesch [Ribbentrop's predecessor as ambassador] and has, if she likes to read them, access to all Secret and Cabinet papers.'

American Ambassador Robert Worth Bingham told Roosevelt: 'Many people here suspect that Mrs. Simpson was in German pay.' Meanwhile, Wallis' dressmaker Anna Wolkoff was sending stolen intelligence to the Nazis through a go-between at the Italian embassy. In 1940, she was sentenced to ten years' penal servitude.

On 7 March 1936, when Hitler sent German troops into the demilitarized Rhineland in violation of the Treaty of Versailles, the British response was muted. Edward was given the credit for this. Ribbentrop told

Hitler that the king had sent 'a directive to the British government that no matter how the details of the affair are dealt with, complications of a serious nature are in no circumstances to be allowed to develop'.

Edward told the German ambassador: 'I sent for the prime minister and gave him a piece of my mind. I told the old so-and-so that I would abdicate if he made war. There was a frightful scene. But you needn't worry. There won't be a war.'

Delighted, the ambassador said: 'I've done it. I've outwitted them all. There won't be a war … we've done it. It's magnificent. I must inform Berlin immediately.'

'At last, the king of England will not intervene,' said Hitler. 'He is keeping his promise.'

Ernest Simpson then decided that he wanted a divorce, so that he could marry Mary Raffray. This would leave Wallis free to marry Edward. Baldwin told the king he could not marry Mrs Simpson as she was a divorcee and he was the head of the Church of England. Princess Stephanie suggested a morganatic marriage, with the support of Ribbentrop, who was desperate to keep Edward on the throne. This proposal was also rejected.

Once the news broke in the British press on 3 December 1936, Edward was forced to abdicate, though Wallis begged him not to, then fled to France.

Alan Don, chaplain to the Archbishop of Canterbury, thought that Edward 'is sexually abnormal which may account for the hold Mrs. S. has over him'. Others speculated that the attraction was the 'Shanghai Squeeze' or the 'Singapore Grip' she had learnt in the Far East. The joke circulated that, while girls could pick up pennies that way, Wallis could pick up a sovereign.

On 10 December, Edward VIII signed the abdication papers. The following evening, he made the famous radio broadcast, saying: 'I have found it impossible to carry the heavy burden of responsibility and to discharge my duties as King as I would wish to do without the help and support of the woman I love.'

On news of the abdication, 500 of Oswald Mosley's Blackshirts from the British Union of Fascists gathered outside Buckingham Palace, giving the fascist salute and shouting, 'We want Edward.'

Edward VIII and Wallis Simpson in 1936.

While his brother, the Duke of York, succeeded to the throne as George VI, the newly-styled Duke of Windsor left for Austria. Detectives in France reported that Wallis intended to move on to Germany – and Edward was sure to follow.

Hitler was upset by the abdication and blamed Bolsheviks, Jews and Freemasons – even Churchill, who had supported the king's marriage to Wallis Simpson.

Although he was out of the country, Edward tried to influence his brother by letter and phone. George stopped taking his calls. One of new Prime Minister Neville Chamberlain's keys advisors, Sir Horace Wilson, wrote of Mrs Simpson: 'It must not be assumed that she has abandoned hope of becoming Queen of England. It is known that she has limitless ambition, including a desire to interfere in politics; she has been in touch with the Nazi movement and has definite ideas as to dictatorship.'

The wedding took place on 3 June 1937 at the Château de Candé, which was owned by the Franco-American businessman Charles Bedaux. After his German companies were seized in 1934, Bedaux leased a schloss in Berchtesgaden and set about ingratiating himself with the Nazi leadership. When Hitler invited the newly-weds to Germany, Bedaux set up the trip. The details were thrashed out when the duke met Princess Stephanie's lover, Hitler's adjutant Fritz Wiedermann, at the Ritz hotel in Paris.

When the Windsors arrived at Friedrichstrasse station in Berlin on 11 October 1937, the place was bedecked with Union Jacks, alternating with swastikas, while the band played 'God Save the King' and the crowd cried 'Heil Edward'.

With an *SS* guard, the Windsors were driven to the Hotel Kaiserhof where they were greeted by Nazi members singing a song especially written by Propaganda Minister Joseph Goebbels. Then they were taken to Göring's country estate, where they met Mussolini, Nazi-sympathizing pioneer airman Charles Lindbergh and former US President Herbert Hoover, as well as the head of the Luftwaffe himself, whose wife remarked that Wallis would have cut a good figure on the throne of England.

On a tour of Munich, Nuremberg, Stuttgart and Dresden, they met Himmler, Rudolf Hess, Goebbels and Ribbentrop. Carl Eduard, Duke of Saxe-Coburg and Gotha, and the rest of the German aristocracy turned out for a gala dinner in Nuremberg.

Greeted by a guard of honour of the *SS* Death's Head Division at a training school in Pomerania, the duke gave a Nazi salute. He gave a second one when he met Hitler at the Berghof on 22 October. Everyone, including Hitler, addressed the duchess as 'Your Royal Highness'.

The Duke and Duchess of Windsor meet Hitler in 1937.

The duke had a private conversation with Hitler that lasted 50 minutes. Afterwards, Hitler and the duke exchanged salutes. Hitler also remarked that the duchess would have made a good queen.

Flushed from this success, Bedaux planned a tour of the US, which would include a visit to the White House. The aim was to launch the duke as an ambassador for world peace, which was simply a cloak for Nazi ambitions. But Bedaux did not realize how unpopular his views had become in the US. He slunk out of the country and the tour had to be cancelled.

War broke out on 3 September 1939. The following month, the rumour circulated in Germany that George VI had abdicated and that Edward was back on the throne. Instead, the Windsors were plucked from a rented villa in Cap d'Antibes and returned to England on the destroyer HMS *Kelly*. In London, Churchill gave the former king a tour of the Secret Room in the basement of the Admiralty where the positions of the British and enemy fleets were recorded hourly. Aghast, the Unionist MP Lord Balniel said: 'He is too irresponsible a chatterbox to be entrusted with confidential information which will be passed on to Wally at the dinner table.'

The duke was assigned to the British Military Mission in France as liaison officer. He spotted the inadequacy of the anti-tank defences in the Ardennes. While the Allies took no notice of his report, the information got back to the Germans. Charles Bedaux regularly had dinner with the Windsors and told Hitler that the duchess was passing classified military information that she had gleaned from her husband over the dinner table.

According to an FBI report, the duchess was still in contact with Ribbentrop. 'Because of their high official position, the duchess was obtaining a variety of information concerning the British and French government activities that she was passing on to the Germans,' it said.

With the German Army overrunning northern France, the Windsors headed for Spain, where newspapers were still reporting that the Duke of Windsor had been returned to the throne and was making peace. Hitler and Ribbentrop asked the Spanish government to delay the duke and Wallis in Spain long enough for 'secret contacts and peace talks'. The German foreign ministry considered him 'the only Englishman who Hitler would negotiate any peace terms with, the logical director of England's destiny after the war'. Edward too believed that Britain could only avoid defeat by making peace with Germany.

On 2 July, the Windsors were allowed to leave Spain. They drove to Lisbon, where the duke avoided the British embassy, fearing he would be arrested if he put a foot inside. Churchill decided that the Windsors could be sidelined by making the duke the governor of the Bahamas. Meanwhile, the Germans did everything they could to lure them back to Spain, even sending Walter Schellenberg. There were fears that the duke might be kidnapped or assassinated and bodyguards were sent from Scotland Yard to travel with him and his wife.

In the Bahamas, the Windsors maintained contact with pro-Nazi American businessman Axel Wenner-Gren. The Windsors sailed to Florida on board Wenner-Gren's yacht, where they joined President Roosevelt for lunch. This was merely a courtesy on the part of the president, but the duke still considered himself a man of influence, telling Roosevelt that, if the president brokered peace between Britain and Germany, he would support him. Roosevelt took no notice, citing Mrs Simpson's dalliance with Ribbentrop, the red boxes left open at Fort Belvedere and the duke's casual attitude to secret plans when he was a liaison officer in France.

Prior to Pearl Harbor, the Duke of Windsor was the poster boy for American isolationists. It was even suspected that he was conspiring with American industrialists who wanted to overthrow democracy in the US and supplant it with fascism. Hoover reported that the duke still had hopes of returning to the throne if Germany won the war.

The Windsors remained confined to the Bahamas until the war in Europe was over. George VI then launched a series of secret missions in Germany to recover sensitive material, including Ribbentrop's file on the Windsors. But the Americans had copies and there were wrangles between the UK and US about whether they should be published. When they finally saw the light of day in 1957, the duke declared the documents implicating him were 'in part complete fabrications, and in part gross distortions of the truth'.

WARTIME WITCHCRAFT

It is well known that Adolf Hitler was obsessed with the occult. His interest began in his twenties when he met a young man called Adolf Lanz, a failed Cistercian monk, who changed his name to Dr Jörg Lanz von Liebenfels. Lanz became a disciple of German mystic Guido von List, who worshipped the Nordic god of war, Woden. During the 1870s, von List had a huge following in Germany and one of the symbols he used in his ceremonies was a hooked cross, the ancient symbol of good fortune known as the swastika. Von List's group evolved into the Thule Society, a pagan group that restricted its membership to high-ranking German Army officers and the professional classes. Meanwhile, Lanz began the Order of the New Templars at the ramshackle Werfenstein Castle on the banks of the Danube. From the flagpole of the castle, he flew a flag with the swastika on it.

Lanz had a number of wealthy and intellectual followers, but none was more fanatical than Hitler. He avidly read Lanz's outpourings in the cult's magazine, *Ostara*, which was devoted to the occult and racial mysticism.

When the Nazi Party was in its infancy, Hitler decided that it should have a symbol to rival the Communist Party's hammer and sickle. Another occultist, Friedrich Kohn, came up with a suggestion. Kohn belonged to the Thule Society, which believed that there was a worldwide Jewish conspiracy, underpinned by occult practices, and the only way to fight it was for Nordic Freemasonry to respond in kind. He suggested a black swastika, symbolizing the triumph of Aryan will, on a white disc, symbolizing racial purity, with a red background, symbolizing blood. Hitler agreed, only he turned the swastika back to front in what has been interpreted as a black magic gesture. It is that reversed swastika that became the emblem of the Nazi Party.

Another believer in the occult who was influential in the Third Reich was Karl Haushofer, father of Rudolf Hess's friend, Albrecht. Born in 1869 in Bavaria, Haushofer came from a military family and, after graduating from Munich University, he joined the German Army. In the early years of the 20th century, he became interested in mysticism and travelled to India and the Far East. He became convinced that the Indo-Germanic people had originated in Central Asia and that it was they who gave nobility and greatness to the world. In Japan, he also joined a secret Buddhist society. During World War I, it is said that his ability to predict where shells would fall was uncanny. He was promoted to the rank of general.

After the war, he returned to Munich University and began teaching his own theory of the 'Science of Geopolitics'. This was thinly disguised nationalist propaganda. He promoted the idea that it was the destiny of the German people to rule Europe and Asia. The heartland of Central Asia was, of course, the Indo-Germanic people's homeland and must be recovered. It would be the centre of unassailable world power. He ran a journal called the *Geopolitical Review*, where he expounded his views of Aryan superiority. He also said that on his travels he had discovered a race of supermen who lived in a vast cavern beneath the Himalayas in a place called Agharti. Similar ideas had been put forward by the Rosicrucians, an esoteric and mystical order that originated in the early 17th century who had themselves influenced the Order of the Golden Dawn, the late-19th-century occult and magical group whose followers included Sherlock Holmes creator Sir Arthur Conan Doyle, infamous black magic practitioner Aleister Crowley, and the Irish poet W. B. Yeats.

One of Haushofer's students was Rudolf Hess, who became his assistant. When Hess and Hitler were jailed for their failed putsch against the Bavarian government in 1923, Haushofer visited Hess in prison and met Hitler. He began visiting Hitler daily and many of Haushofer's ideas were incorporated in *Mein Kampf.* Hess later said that Haushofer was the secret Master Magician behind the Reich. His ideas of 'cones of power' were incorporated in the staging of the Nuremberg rallies and he brought Buddhist teachers called lamas from Tibet and members of the Green Dragon Society from Japan to Germany to lend the war effort mystical backing.

Heinrich Himmler, head of the *SS*, was another believer in the occult. The *SS* used occult practices and worshipped Woden in ceremonies in the castle at Wewelsburg in northwest Germany where Himmler had built a temple known as the Hall of the Dead.

However, during World War II, such harmless practices as astrology and palmistry were banned in all German occupied countries. Even occult organizations such as the Thule Society and the German Order, who had backed Hitler from the outset, were outlawed. Occult practice was to be confined to those at the top of the Nazi Party.

Whatever help the occult may have lent Hitler, his experiment in pure evil failed. But even in defeat, Hitler did not give up his belief. He delayed his own suicide until the pagan festival of *Walpurgisnacht*, the night of the witches, 30 April 1945.

During World War II, there were some strange goings-on in Britain too. On the afternoon of 18 April 1943, three boys were looking for eggs in birds' nests in Hagley Wood in Worcestershire. The woods were part of the estate of Hagley Hall, the ancestral home of Lord Cobham. It was late in the afternoon and the light was already failing when they decided to have a look in an old wych elm. One of them clambered up it. Hidden under the spindly branches, he discovered a large hole in the trunk – just the place a bird might nest. Peering down into the cavity, he saw what looked like a grimacing face.

He took a stick and prodded at it. Slowly it dawned on the boy that what he was prodding was a skull. Shaken by the experience, the boy and his two companions ran home and told their parents. They informed the police. By then it was dark and it was too late to examine the tree. So, the local bobby, Sergeant Skerratt, placed a guard on the tree overnight.

In the morning, detectives from Worcestershire CID turned up. They set about examining the hollow in the tree. First, they managed to retrieve the skull. Then they found a spine, a shoulder blade and some human ribs, still with pieces of rotten clothing clinging to them. And at the bottom of the hole, they found a single crepe-soled shoe.

The tree and the surrounding area were photographed and Sergeant Skerratt took detailed measurements of the hollow. It was about 1 m (3.3 ft) off the ground and it was just 60 cm (2 ft) across at its widest. The trunk itself had been cut off at about 1.67 m (5.5 ft) and the resulting tangle of branches would have made it very difficult to shove a body into the hollow. The surrounding area was cordoned off and a thorough search was made. A shin bone was found knotted in the roots of a sapling nearby. A little further away, detectives found a buried hand.

Most of the skeleton was eventually found and remnants of the victim's clothing were discovered strewn through the undergrowth. The job of reconstructing the body fell to West Midlands pathologist Professor J. M. Webster. The local newspaper, the *Wolverhampton Express and Star*, billed him as 'as famous as any figure who ever helped solve a crime excepting, perhaps, Sherlock Holmes'.

Webster had set up Britain's first forensic science laboratory in Sheffield in 1929 and he had established the West Midlands forensic laboratory before the war. Meticulously, he pieced the body back together and built up a remarkable picture of the victim. She was a brown-haired woman, around 1.5 m (5 ft) tall and about 35 years old when she died. She had a cheap ring on her wedding finger. The words 'Rolled Gold' were stamped on it. She was wearing blue crepe-soled shoes, a cloth skirt with a zip and a peach-coloured taffeta underskirt, along with a dark blue knitted woollen cardigan, fastened with a light blue belt. Professor Webster drew up a detailed artist's impression of the victim and a dummy was prepared to give the police a more accurate idea of the missing woman. The front teeth in the victim's lower jaw were noticeably irregular. This should have made her readily identifiable. However, no dentist who had treated her came forward. Detailed notices in all the dental journals elicited not a single response.

Professor Webster estimated that the victim had been dead for around 18 months when discovered. Part of her clothing had been stuffed deep into the cavity of the jaw. This had happened before she had died and Professor Webster believed that the woman had probably asphyxiated. But he could not be sure. Her body had been jammed into the hollow in the tree, feet first, shortly after she had died – certainly before rigor mortis had set in. She could not have squeezed in there when she was alive.

The inquest opened on 28 April 1943 at North Worcestershire Coroner's Court in Stourbridge. The verdict was 'murder by person or persons unknown'. This did not help the police with their enquiries. They were still no closer to finding out who the dead woman was, let alone the identity of who had killed her. They tried checking through their missing persons files. But the bombings and wartime disruption made this a monumental and ultimately fruitless task. At the same time, they checked with clothing manufacturers in the hope that they could trace the woman through the distribution chain.

Her unusual blue crepe-soled shoes seemed to offer some hope in this regard. The police found the manufacturer and tracked down all but four pairs of that type of shoe sold. But none of the purchasers gave a clue to the identity of the unknown victim.

Searching back in their records, the police discovered that two men – a teacher and a businessman – had reported hearing screams emanating from Hagley Wood in July 1941. A constable had assisted the two men in searching the woods, but nothing suspicious had been found. The date of this report would be consistent with Professor Webster's estimated time of death. On the other hand, there was not a shred of other evidence to tie the two events together. Another report showed that gypsies had been camping in the woods at that time. The police had stepped in following a minor domestic dispute. The hypothesis that the victim was a gypsy was appealing. It would explain the difficulty in tracing her. But enquiries among the Romany community drew a blank.

The police had only one thing to go on. Although the victim was clearly an outsider, the perpetrator must have had good local knowledge. The wych elm was less than 800 m (0.5 miles) from the main road from Kidderminster to Birmingham in an area popular with picnickers, hikers and courting couples. But the hollow was so well hidden it seemed inconceivable that anyone who had not spent a great deal of time in Hagley Wood would have happened upon it by chance. But why would anyone choose such an inconvenient and inefficient way of concealing a corpse? The victim had to have been dismembered directly after the murder, the bulk of the body jammed into an awkward confined space and the rest of the corpse and clothing disposed of piecemeal. Why not simply bury the body in one piece?

Letters to the local papers suggested that the woman's murder was part of a black magic ritual. Mysterious messages were also chalked on the walls of empty buildings in Wolverhampton, Old Hill and Halesowen. They said: 'Who put Bella down the wych elm, Hagley Wood?' Sometimes the graffiti artist used the name 'Luebella'. Both names are diminutives of 'Elizabeth' and are commonly associated with witchcraft.

Hagley Wood had a reputation as a witches' haunt. But the police found no current indications of occult activity. However, there are plenty of superstitions surrounding corpses and trees. According to folklore, the spirit of a witch could be confined in a hollow tree. In ancient times, blood sacrifices were offered to damaged trees and the wych elm in Hagley Wood was actually only a living stump, the main trunk having been severed. Another indication that this had been an occult killing was that one hand had been cut off and buried some distance from the corpse. There is no rational reason why it was removed. Despite the tight squeeze, it could have been fitted into the hollow. However, in occult practices, the severed hand of a corpse – especially one taken from a hanged man on the gallows – has magical powers. It can be used to find treasure, paralyse enemies, charm locks open and perform supernatural robberies. If a lighted candle is put in the hand, or one of the fingers is set alight, light from the flame is supposed to put all those who see it into a death-like sleep. To have these mystical properties, the 'hand of glory' has to be dried and pickled in a special way. The name comes from the French *main de gloire* and is related to the mandragora plant which has narcotic properties.

Interesting though all that may be, it did not get the police any closer to finding the identity of the victim or the killer. Their only hope was to find the author of the messages chalked up on the walls. These had been carefully printed in capital letters about 8 cm (3 in) high and must have taken some time to complete. But the perpetrator was never seen and no one acting suspiciously was ever reported in the vicinity. The investigation of the corpse in Hagley Wood had ground to a halt.

Interest in the case was rekindled nearly two years later with the mysterious death of a 74-year-old farm labourer called Charles Walton. He lived not too far away in the quaint village of Lower Quinton in Warwickshire. Partially crippled by rheumatism, Walton could not walk without the aid of a stick, but on the morning of 14 February 1945 he set off to do some hedge-laying for local farmers. At 9 am he left the picturesque thatched cottage he shared with his niece, Edith, and trudged off on the mile or so to the fields below Meon Hill, a lonely spot. He carried with him a pitchfork and a hedge-trimmer's slash-hook.

Walton was a man of regular habits. He would return home each day at 4 pm for his tea. So, when he had not appeared by 6 pm, Edith became concerned that he had had an accident. With neighbour Harry Beasley, she went looking for the old man. But they could not find him. As it grew dark, they became more and more worried. Edith got in touch with her uncle's employer, Alfred Potter. By torchlight, they went to search Meon Hill. Late that night, they found the old man's body stretched out under a willow tree. Potter went over to examine it and he shouted over to Edith: 'Don't come any nearer! You mustn't look at this!'

Potter stayed by the body, while Beasley escorted Edith back to her cottage and called the police. When they turned up, they were horrified by what they found. Walton was pinned to the ground by the neck. He had been run through by his own pitchfork. The prongs protruded a full 15 cm (6 in) into the ground. It took two policemen to pull it out. The sign of the cross had been cut into Walton's chest with the slash-hook. The hook itself was embedded in a huge gash in the victim's throat. And there were gashes along the outsides of his arms, as if he had tried to defend himself. The old man's walking stick was found nearby. It was bloodstained and had also been used as a weapon by the attacker.

Professor J. M. Webster, the pathologist who had reconstructed the body found in Hagley Wood, was called in to make an initial examination at the scene of the crime. Then Walton's body was carried back to the village on a five-barred gate.

Superintendent Simmons from Stratford-upon-Avon, just 13 km (8 miles) to the north, was initially put in charge of the investigation. He imagined that his task would be relatively simple. There were only 500 people in Lower Quinton – there could be few secrets in such a small community and it would be difficult for the killer to hide. However, there were few clues at the scene of the crime, no obvious motive and the villagers were deeply suspicious of outsiders. Interviews revealed only that Charles Walton was a reclusive man. He had few friends and there was no reason to suspect he had any enemies. The report in the local newspaper, the *Stratford-upon-Avon Herald*, claimed that it was a random murder committed by 'a lunatic or someone maddened by drink'. The case was so baffling that, within two days of the murder, Detective Superintendent Alec Spooner of the Warwickshire CID called in the legendary Fabian of the Yard.

Superintendent Robert Fabian was Britain's most famous policeman. His career at Scotland Yard spanned 29 years and included spells as head of the Flying Squad and the Vice Squad. After the war, Fabian appeared frequently on television. Feature films were made of his most famous cases and he made lecture tours of South Africa and the United States, where he was given the freedom of New Orleans. In 1960, he was decorated with the Police Medal for Gallantry, after defusing a bomb in London.

Fabian hurried to Lower Quinton, arriving at dawn on 16 February. But he found that local policemen had already combed the murder site, trampling any clues and making it impossible to reconstruct what had happened. And the clumsy removal of the pitchfork and the slash hook had obliterated any fingerprints that may have been on them. But this was wartime and Fabian had special techniques available to him that would not have been feasible before.

He called the Royal Air Force base at Leamington. They sent out an Avro Anson reconnaissance plane to take aerial photographs of the area. These were detailed enough to pick out footprints and bloodstains, but Fabian had a more prosaic use for these reconnaissance pictures. He used them to construct a large-scale map so that he could trace the movements of everyone from the village on the day of the murder.

So far, the local residents had not been very forthcoming. Only Alfred Potter admitted to seeing Charles Walton at work that day, though Meon Hill was open country and anyone working out there would have been clearly visible. With the map and details of everyone's movements, Fabian might be able to jog a few memories in the village. As well as being deeply suspicious of the police, the villagers had their own theory of who the killer might be. They claimed that there was something deeply un-English about the way Walton had been killed. Plainly foreigners were to blame. Luckily, there were plenty to hand.

By 1945, there were over 40,000 prisoners of war being held in Britain – with hundreds of thousands of others being held in camps in the United States, Canada, North Africa and on mainland Europe. As the war dragged on to its conclusion, security got pretty lax. Few if any prisoners wanted to return to the war and no PoW held in Britain ever got back to Germany. In fact, the only recorded case of a German making a 'home run' was from Canada, when the United States was still neutral and the border porous.

However, trouble in prisoner-of-war camps was not uncommon. A week before the murder, there was a break-out in northwest England. Seven Germans got away. They were quickly recaptured. In the process, one was killed and four were injured. And there was a break-out at Atherstone in Warwickshire a month later.

There was a prisoner-of-war camp at Long Marston, just 3 km (2 miles) from Lower Quinton. It would have been easy enough for a PoW to slip out of the camp, commit the murder and slip back in again without being spotted. Local police had been to the camp the night after the murder. But there were 1,043 prisoners of war there – Germans, Italians, Ukrainians and

Slavs. The prospect of interviewing them all was daunting. With nothing else to go on, Fabian called in Special Branch language expert Detective Sergeant David Saunders and began a long round of interviews. Eventually, they came up with a suspect. Several of the prisoners had seen an Italian serviceman desperately trying to scrub bloodstains out of his coat. When questioned, the Italian stubbornly refused to talk. Plainly he had something to hide. His coat was sent away for forensic examination.

A tin watch was missing from Walton's body and Fabian had called in a mine-detecting team from the Royal Engineers. So far, they had drawn a blank, so Fabian put them to work in the area where the Italian had been seen acting suspiciously. What they unearthed were some home-made animal snares. The blood on his coat proved to be that of a rabbit. The Italian had been supplementing his meagre PoW rations with a bit of poaching. That's why he had kept quiet.

Fabian was quickly running out of any reasonable line of enquiry. However, a fellow officer mentioned that there was a bizarre precedent for the killing. In 1875, an old woman called Ann Turner had been killed by one John Haywood. According to the report at the time, he had stabbed her with a pitchfork before 'slashing her throat with a billhook in the form of a cross'. Surely this could not be a coincidence? Then, one evening, Fabian was walking up near the crime site on Meon Hill. A huge black dog came bounding past him and disappeared down the hill. A few minutes later, Fabian happened on a farm lad and asked him if he had lost a black dog. The boy blanched and ran away from the detective in panic.

That night, Fabian mentioned this intriguing incident in the local pub, the College Arms. Villagers told him that there was a local legend surrounding a ghostly black dog. Its appearance, they said, was supposed to be a harbinger of death. Many years before, a 14-year-old ploughboy had seen the dog nine times. The last time he saw it, it suddenly turned into a headless woman as it rushed past him, emitting an eerie rustling sound. The following day, the boy's sister died. Superstitious twaddle, surely. But with nothing else to go on, Fabian had the story checked out. He discovered that such an incident had indeed been reported in 1885. And the ploughboy who had seen the dog was none other than Charles Walton – who now, 60 years later, had been murdered on Meon Hill.

Up to this point, the locals had been wary. Now they clammed up completely. When Fabian visited the College Arms before, the locals might have given him the time of day. Now the place fell silent and, when Fabian walked in, everyone else walked out. The enquiry hit a brick wall. The mere mention of Charles Walton's name would prompt talk of a dead heifer, failed crops and veiled mentions of the evil eye. There was also talk of the Rollright Stones.

A few miles from the village of Lower Quinton are 70 or so standing stones arranged in a circle that has exactly the same diameter as the inner circle of Stonehenge. The local legend is that they were formed when a witch confronted an invading army. She transformed the leader into the 'King Stone' – which was the largest of the group – and the king's followers became the rest of the ring of stones, known as the 'Whispering Knights'. It is said that the stones periodically come to life and drink at the nearby stream, that their exact number can never be counted and that they can induce fertility in a barren woman. It was whispered that Charles Walton had seen witches dancing by them when he was a boy. Indeed, the Rollright Stones have undoubtedly been a focus for occult activity. In the 1970s, the police found the charred remains of a puppy there after one midnight ceremony.

The Rollright Stones – a centre of witchcraft in the area?

Disquieting things began happening around the village. A calf died mysteriously at a local farm. A police car ran over a hound in one of the narrow lanes near the village. A black dog was found hanged by its collar from a bush near where Walton had been murdered. Meanwhile, police enquiries were getting nowhere. Every one of the villagers was interviewed. In addition to the questioning of the prisoners of war, efforts had been made to track down gypsies and tinkers who might have been in the area at the time. They were detained as far away as Somerset and Salisbury. But no one could shed any light on the murder.

On 20 February, the inquest into Walton's death was opened, but, after a brief hearing it was adjourned for a month. However, it was revealed that his clothing had been tampered with. Many of the villagers, it seemed, believed that Walton had a money belt. Fabian believed that money was the motive for the crime. Edith Walton said that her uncle had lent Alfred Potter substantial sums of money. The war had hurt Potter's business and his farm was in dire financial straits. Potter was supposedly a pillar of the community. He was a member of the British Legion and a sidesman (a kind of churchwarden) at the local church. He was also a cricket fan and a race-goer, and was known to be violent when drunk. Walton was on his land when he was killed and Potter had a compelling motive to see him dead: the repayment of Walton's loans was long overdue. The problem was that there was no documentary proof that the loans had ever been made; the evidence against Potter was not strong enough for charges to be laid against him.

At the second inquest, Potter was cross-questioned by the coroner. Not only was Potter the only person to have seen Walton at work on the day of his death, there were huge inconsistencies in his story. At first, he said he had seen Walton at about 12.30 pm from a distance of about 450 m (1,476 ft). He had been in his shirtsleeves, Potter said. But Walton had been wearing a short-sleeved shirt that day. Potter admitted drinking in the College Arms on the day of the murder and later said that he had been helping another farmer rescue a heifer that had fallen in a ditch at the time he said he had seen Walton. But the coroner excused these contradictions because of the shock Potter had suffered in discovering the body. As the police had no concrete evidence to offer, the coroner found that Charles Walton had been 'murdered by person or persons unknown'.

Fabian remained convinced that Potter was the culprit and that he manufactured the evidence of occult activity to disguise the financial motives for the murder. It also ensured the silence of other superstitious villagers. However, other occult experts believed that there was more to it than that.

The murder had occurred on 14 February which, that year, was not only St Valentine's Day but Ash Wednesday, too. It was also the Druidic festival of Imbolc (or, in the Christian calendar, Candlemas). Imbolc/Candlemas is one of the four 'Greater Sabbats', the festival days on which Wiccan pagan rituals are performed when the links between the physical world and the supernatural realm are at their closest. With dark talk of failed crops and heifers dying mysteriously, the idea was floated that Walton had been slaughtered as part of a fertility ritual. Others speculated that Walton himself was part of an occult group and had been killed because of it.

Distinguished Egyptologist and occult expert Dr Margaret Murray – the author of *The Witch Cult in Western Europe* and *The God of the Witches* – visited Lower Quinton in 1950. Belief in the occult there was very deep, she concluded. Walton, she believed, had been a blood sacrifice and his killer was a countryman following country ways. But Dr Murray agreed with Fabian in one respect. Both were certain that the people of Lower Quinton knew who had killed Charles Walton. They were just not saying.

Margaret Murray also made a study of the case of the body in Hagley Wood and became convinced that the murdered woman was 'another victim of the devil worshippers'. Others ridiculed the idea of occult involvement. 'I think she was a gypsy and that she was tried and condemned by her tribe of Romanies,' the local churchwarden said.

Following Dr Murray's investigations, the *Wolverhampton Express and Star* took up the case again. A journalist calling himself 'Quaestor' wrote a series of articles linking the body in Hagley Wood with the murder of Charles Walton. He traced two of the boys who had been bird egg hunting the day the corpse was found. Both were afraid of returning to the wych elm. The third boy had apparently died of shock after their ghastly find.

Following the publication of Quaestor's articles, the *Express and Star* received a stream of letters, one of which came from a woman calling herself 'Anna'. She said that the victim had been a Dutch woman and that the 'person responsible for the crime died insane in 1942'. This was an attractive theory as it would explain why the police could not trace her clothing or dental records.

The police interviewed 'Anna' and were clearly impressed by her story. They made further enquiries in Holland. But no arrest was ever made and the victim's identity was never revealed. Like the murder of Charles Walton in Lower Quinton, the Hagley Wood case remains officially unsolved.

Nevertheless, author Donald McCormick believes he has the answer. After a detailed study of the case, he came to the conclusion that the Dutch woman mentioned by 'Anna' was an agent codenamed 'Clara' who was parachuted into the Kidderminster area in mid-1941 and then vanished. McCormick's theory was that 'Clara' was related to Johannes Marinus Dronkers, a Dutch spy working for the Germans, who was executed by the British in 1942.

It was known that 'Clara' Dronkers was interested in astrology and she may have been fleeing from *Aktion Hess*, the purge launched by Hitler that followed the flight of his deputy Rudolf Hess to Scotland in 1941. As part of that action, astrologers throughout Germany and the occupied nations were rounded up and sent to concentration camps.

THE CAMBRIDGE FIVE

While the war was going on there was another conspiracy happening at the heart of the British Establishment. This was a ring of spies in the security services who were handing over state secrets – not to the enemy in Berlin, but to the Russians in Moscow, ostensibly Britain's allies.

Five young men of impeccable backgrounds had been recruited by Soviet intelligence while they were studying at Cambridge University in the 1930s. They were Donald Maclean, Guy Burgess, Harold 'Kim' Philby, Anthony Blunt and John Cairncross. Watching the rise of the Fascists in Italy and the Nazis in Germany, they were persuaded that the only force that could stand against Hitler's dream of world domination was Communism. Consequently, they were prepared to conspire against their own country and go to work for the Soviet Union.

The Cambridge Five worked their way into high positions in the British security services and leaked thousands of documents to their masters in Moscow – so many, that Soviet intelligence thought that they must be triple agents leaking disinformation for MI5 or MI6. They were particularly suspicious of Kim Philby. His youthful Communist sympathies had been so open and obvious that, the Soviets reasoned, it was improbable that the British government would ever trust him with state secrets.

Soviet agents has been active in the UK from the early 1920s, but they quickly realized that recruiting Communists from among the working class was of no use to them; they needed to attract people from the upper echelons of British society – people who could land prestigious civil service jobs and infiltrate the highest levels of the British state. Naturally, the Soviets turned to Oxford and Cambridge Universities.

In 1931 24-year-old Anthony Blunt was a don at Trinity College, Cambridge, where he met 20-year-old student Guy Burgess. They were both gay, but Blunt denied they were ever lovers. Blunt later said he was not then interested in politics, despite the events unfolding in Europe, but Burgess was. 'I found that Cambridge had been hit by Marxism and that most of my friends among my junior contemporaries – including Guy Burgess – had either joined the Communist Party or were at least very close to it politically,' Blunt later admitted. 'Eventually, largely owing to the influence of Guy Burgess … I realized that one could no longer stand aside. The issue of Fascism, as posed by the advent to power of Hitler and later by the Spanish Civil War, became so urgent that the Ivory Tower no longer provided adequate refuge.'

Blunt considered joining the Communist Party, until Burgess revealed the startling secret that he had resigned from it on instructions from the Comintern – the Soviet-led organization that advocated the spread of world Communism – who wanted him working for them from inside the government or the BBC. Blunt said that Burgess convinced him to join him in this work, though he claimed that he was so politically naïve that he did not realize that this would commit him to clandestine political activity. However, he visited the Soviet Union in 1933.

After he was recruited, Blunt became a Soviet 'talent spotter' and is thought to have identified the other three members of the Cambridge Five as potential spies. When war broke out, he joined the British Army and was posted to the Intelligence Corps. From there, he went to MI5, where he had access to the Ultra decrypts from Bletchley Park – which he passed on with other secret documents and intercepts of *Wehrmacht* radio traffic on the Eastern Front to the Soviets, as well as details of German spy rings operating in the Soviet Union. The Soviet Union was an ally of Britain at the time, but that's not to say that Blunt's actions were acceptable. They certainly were not authorized.

After university, Guy Burgess joined the BBC as a producer, before becoming a full-time MI6 officer. He then joined the Foreign Office in

1944. This gave him access to secret information on all aspects of Britain's foreign policy during the critical post-1945 period at the beginning of the Cold War. It is estimated that Burgess passed copies of several thousand documents to his Soviet controllers. In 1950, he was appointed Second Secretary to the British embassy in Washington, D.C. A serious alcoholic, he was sent home after repeated misbehaviour.

Blunt and Burgess were both members of an exclusive debating society called The Apostles. Another member was Donald Maclean, another student at Trinity. At university, he became a Communist and visited Moscow. He was recruited by Soviet intelligence. After claiming to have become disenchanted with Communism, he joined the Foreign Office and began passing documents to the Soviet Union. In 1944, he was posted to the British embassy in Washington, D.C., where he became first secretary. This gave him access to atomic secrets, which he gave to the Soviets. In 1948, he was moved to the embassy in Cairo. He began drinking heavily and had to be returned to a desk job in London.

Another student at Trinity was Kim Philby. He had canvassed on behalf of the Labour Party, but became disillusioned when its leader Ramsay MacDonald formed a national government with the Tories in 1931. Gradually, he became more left-wing.

'On my very last day at Cambridge I decided that I would become a Communist,' he said.

He joined a Communist group in Paris, then moved on to an underground organization smuggling socialists and Communists out of Austria. Back in London, he was courted by Soviet agents. A Czech named Arnold Deutsch had been sent to University College, London, under the cover of a research appointment, to recruit the brightest students from Britain's top universities. Philby came to Deutsch's attention due to his activities in Vienna. He met up with Deutsch – who was calling himself Otto – in Regent's Park. Philby then put Deutsch on to Maclean and Burgess.

Philby became a journalist and made many trips to Berlin. He and Burgess joined the Anglo-German Fellowship to disguise their Communist leanings. Covering the Spanish Civil War as a freelance writer, he became a correspondent for *The Times*. There, he began working for both Soviet and British intelligence.

In 1938, a former Soviet intelligence officer named Walter Krivitsky defected. Questioned by MI5, he revealed that two Soviet intelligence agents had penetrated the Foreign Office and a third had worked as a journalist for a British newspaper during the civil war in Spain. No connection with Burgess, Maclean and Philby was made at the time, and Krivitsky was found shot dead in a hotel room in Washington, D.C., the following year.

Philby's controller in Madrid, Alexander Orlov, also defected. To protect his family, who were still living in the USSR, Orlov said nothing about Philby. Consequently, Philby continued working for *The Times* until 1940, when Burgess recommended him to MI6. Burgess and Philby worked together in Section D, the sabotage section, until it was absorbed into SOE.

Philby provided Stalin with advanced warning of Hitler's proposed attack on the Soviet Union. This was ignored as possibly British provocation in the light of the non-aggression pact between Russia and Germany then in place. He also told his Soviet controller of Japan's intention to strike into Southeast Asia instead of attacking the Soviet Union, as Hitler had urged. This was confirmed by Richard Sorge, a German journalist and Soviet spy in Tokyo, allowing Stalin to move troops from the Far East to defend Moscow after Germany tore up the pact and launched its invasion of the Soviet Union.

By September 1941 Philby was working for Section Five of MI6, which was responsible for offensive counterintelligence. He was put in charge of the subsection that dealt with Spain and Portugal. It kept a watch on the *Abwehr*, which had established a network of posts watching shipping in the Straits of Gibraltar, using infrared detectors when visibility was poor. The British put pressure on the Spanish government to have the posts closed down, otherwise they would cut off oil supplies.

As the war turned in the Allies' favour, it was considered that, after the defeat of Hitler, the Soviet Union would become a threat to the West. Section Nine, which handled anti-Communist activities, was reactivated and Philby became its head. His job was to put agents behind Soviet lines.

Alerted to Britain's hostile intent, Stalin held back British captives liberated from German PoW camps. Some 31,000 British servicemen, along with 20,000 Americans and some French, Belgians and Dutchmen, disappeared into the Gulags, the Soviet network of labour camps.

While the information that Philby provided proved accurate, Moscow was still suspicious when he assured them that no British agents had penetrated Soviet intelligence in London or Moscow. And how could the British have failed to notice the thousands of documents that were being removed from the offices of their security services?

As head of Section Nine, Philby liaised with James Jesus Angleton, a young American counterintelligence officer stationed in London who went on to head the CIA. Early on, Angleton was one of those who voiced their suspicions about Philby.

A Soviet intelligence agent named Konstantin Volkov working as the vice-consul in Istanbul asked for asylum in Britain for himself and his wife, saying he knew of two Soviet agents in the British Foreign Office and one in counterintelligence. Philby was sent to Turkey to handle the defection. By the time he got there, Volkov had been bundled on a plane back to Moscow after Philby had informed his Soviet handlers.

Again, Philby came under suspicion. But Volkov himself had insisted that, for security purposes, all correspondence concerning his defection was sent by diplomatic bag, rather than telegraph, so Philby blamed the tardiness of couriers for this late arrival. It was later discovered that the telephone lines to the British embassy in Ankara had been tapped, which gave him cover.

More suspicions were raised when Igor Gouzenko, a cipher clerk in Ottawa, took political asylum in Canada and gave the Royal Canadian Mounted Police details of agents operating within the British Empire. But Philby was in a position where he could manipulate and close off any investigation.

As head of British intelligence in Turkey, Philby cooperated with Turkey organizing the infiltration of anti-Communist agents into Soviet Armenia and Georgia. They were shot as soon as they crossed the border.

Kim Philby was assigned the task of discovering the identity of the Soviet agent 'Homer'. Several years later it was revealed that Philby was in fact a Russian double agent.

A similar fate lay in store for full-scale landings in Albania organized with the CIA. Philby had no regrets about the deaths.

Philby was then posted to Washington, D.C., as head of the SIS. Liaising with the CIA, he found himself working with James Jesus Angleton again.

In the summer of 1945, a Soviet cipher clerk had reused a code that had only been intended for a single operation while transmitting intelligence traffic. This slip made it possible to break the Soviets' otherwise impregnable codes. The subsequent decrypting of intercepted traffic was known as the Venona Project. It led to the unmasking of Soviet atomic spies Klaus Fuchs, Harry Gold, David Greenglass and Julius and Ethel Rosenberg. It also revealed that documents from the British embassy in Washington, D.C., had been sent to Moscow by an agent codenamed 'Homer', who travelled to New York City to meet his Soviet contact twice a week.

Philby was assigned to discover who Homer was. He knew perfectly well that it was Maclean. He was going through the motions of investigating when Guy Burgess was posted to Washington, D.C., as second secretary. He stayed with Philby. Drinking heavily, Burgess misbehaved and cruised the US capital for homosexual pickups.

Maclean was back in London. Philby had to warn him. In early May 1951, Burgess got three speeding tickets in a single day and was sent back to London. The SIS planned to interrogate Maclean on 28 May 1951. On 23 May, Philby wired Burgess, ostensibly about his having left his Lincoln convertible in the embassy car park, but it was actually a coded message urging Maclean to flee.

On 25 May Burgess drove Maclean to Southampton. Once Maclean's exit plan was put in place, Burgess decided to flee as well. They took a ship to France, then made their way to Moscow. There was uproar about the two defecting diplomats. Suspected of being the informer who had warned them, Philby returned to London to be interrogated by MI5. In July, he resigned from MI6.

After speculation in the press in 1955, Philby was named as the 'third man' in the Burgess–Maclean spy ring. The allegation was then withdrawn and a further investigation cleared Philby. Going on to the offensive, he gave a press conference where he confidently declared that he had never been a Communist.

The following year, Philby moved to Beirut as Middle East correspondent for *The Observer* and *The Economist*. Using this as cover, he resumed working for MI6.

In 1961, Anatoliy Golitsyn, a major in the First Chief Directorate of the KGB, defected to the United States, offering to reveal Soviet agents within American and British intelligence services. Golitsyn, again, named Philby. MI6 agent Nicholas Elliott, a friend of Philby's who had previously believed in his innocence, was sent to Beirut to secure a confession.

Philby admitted everything, but before he signed a confession he disappeared, resurfacing six months later in Moscow where he had been granted political asylum and Soviet citizenship. He died there in 1988.

In the final days of World War II, Anthony Blunt was sent to Germany to recover sensitive material about the royal family, looking particularly for anything concerning the Duke of Windsor. As a reward, he became Surveyor of the King's Pictures. At the same time, he retained his contacts with Soviet agents and continued to pass them gossip from his former MI5 colleagues and documents from Burgess.

With the defection of Burgess and Maclean in May 1951, Blunt also came under suspicion as he and Burgess had been friends since Cambridge. But he was only unmasked in 1963, when an American admitted he had been recruited by Blunt, who then confessed. After being promised immunity from prosecution, he named John Cairncross and others as spies. His confession was kept secret until the publication of Andrew Boyle's book *Climate of Treason* in 1979, when he was publicly shamed in the House of Commons by the prime minister, Margaret Thatcher, and stripped of his knighthood.

John Cairncross was another student at Trinity in the 1930s. He joined the Communist Party in 1936 and was recruited as a Soviet spy. Working first at the Foreign Office, he moved to the Treasury, then the Cabinet Office. In 1942, he moved to Bletchley Park, handling Ultra decrypts, before joining MI6 the following year.

He smuggled transcripts out of Bletchley Park in his trousers, handing them to his Soviet contact in London. Among the 5,832 documents he supplied there were communications with Yugoslav partisans and material concerning the German deployments of Kursk, which helped the Soviets win the crucial battle.

In MI6, Cairncross worked under Kim Philby. After the defections of Burgess and Maclean, Cairncross was questioned by British counterintelligence, but had been trained to resist interrogation. While he had told the Soviets that Britain intended to build atomic weapons, he was never prosecuted. He was not revealed as the 'fifth man' in the Cambridge spy ring until 1990, when KGB defector Oleg Gordievsky named him publicly.

KLAUS FUCHS

While the Cambridge Five were passing on atomic secrets, the Soviet Union already had a man inside the West's bomb project whose efforts allowed them to produce their own atomic bomb in 1949.

Born in 1911 in Germany, Klaus Fuchs studied maths and physics at the Universities of Leipzig and Kiel, where he became involved in student politics. Fearing the rise of Hitler, he joined the Communist Party. He was beaten up and thrown into a river by the Nazis. He moved on to the Kaiser Wilhelm Institute for Physics in Berlin, where Albert Einstein had been director until Hitler came to power.

Fuchs himself went into hiding before fleeing to Britain, where he worked in various academic posts. When war broke out his application to become a British subject had not yet been processed, so he was interned as an enemy alien, first on the Isle of Man and then in Canada.

After being returned to Britain in 1941, he went to work at 'Tube Alloys' – the codename for Britain's atomic bomb programme. Its work convinced the Americans that making an atomic bomb was possible. Fuchs was granted British citizenship and signed the Official Secrets Act.

To escape Germany's bombing raids, the British atomic project was transferred to the United States and became part of the Manhattan Project, a joint US-British-Canadian effort to build an atomic bomb. Working at Columbia University in New York, Fuchs was contacted by Soviet agent Harry Gold.

Klaus Fuchs – an anti-Nazi physicist turned atom spy.

In August 1944, Fuchs was transferred to Los Alamos, continuing his theoretical work. He was one of those who witnessed the Trinity test – the first detonation of an atomic bomb. He went on to work on the hydrogen bomb, a thermonuclear weapon which was immensely more powerful.

The US Atomic Energy Act of 1946 prohibited the transfer of information on nuclear research to any foreign country, including Britain, without explicit official authority. Fuchs was supplying highly classified US information to nuclear scientists in Britain and to his Soviet contacts via Harry Gold.

In August 1946, Fuchs returned to Britain to work on Britain's postwar nuclear weapons programme as head of the Theoretical Physics Division at the Atomic Energy Research Establishment at Harwell. He continued supplying classified information to the Soviets through his case officer, Alexander Feklisov.

In September 1949, Venona decrypts indicated that Fuchs was a spy. The Soviets broke off contact with him and he may have been tipped off by Kim Philby, who was still seeing the intelligence coming out of Venona.

Fuchs was interviewed by MI5 officer William Skardon and told that, if he confessed to his wartime spying activity, he could stay on at Harwell. However, news came through that his father had been made a professor at Leipzig University in Communist East Germany and he was forced to resign. He then confessed all to Skardon. Information he gave on other Soviet spies in the atomic programme led to the arrest of Harry Gold. He turned state's evidence on fellow agents David Greenglass and Julius and Ethel Rosenberg, leading to the Rosenbergs' execution in the electric chair in 1953.

Arrested on 2 February 1950, Fuchs was charged with violations of the Official Secrets Act. Asked why he had spied, Fuchs said that 'Knowledge of atomic research should not be the private property of any one country but should be shared with the rest of the world for the benefit of mankind.'

The information that Fuchs gave the Soviets helped their atomic weapons project, particularly because it told them how uranium could be refined to produce the fissile isotope used in a bomb. Fuchs had given

Gold technical information in January 1945 that had taken two years of experimentation at a cost of $400 million to discover. Fuchs also disclosed the amount of uranium or plutonium the Americans planned to use in each atomic bomb.

Thanks to Fuchs' espionage, the US cancelled a 1950 Anglo-American plan to give Britain American-made atomic bombs, though the British had developed the theoretical basis of the bomb in the first place. Britain went on to develop nuclear weapons on its own account using some of the work provided by Fuchs.

Fuchs was charged with four counts of breaking the Official Secrets Act by 'communicating information to a potential enemy'. He pleaded guilty. His trial lasted less than 90 minutes. A plea for mitigation was entered on the grounds of his state of mind and his desire to assist the Soviets in defeating the Nazis and win the war. He was sentenced to 14 years and stripped of his British citizenship. In 1952, he was visited in prison by Sir William Penney, head of the British H-bomb project.

Fuchs served nine years. When released in 1959, he emigrated to the German Democratic Republic – Communist East Germany – where he resumed his career as a scientist. It is thought that a tutorial Fuchs gave to Qian Sanqiang and other Chinese physicists helped them to develop the first Chinese atomic bomb, which was tested five years later.

Fuchs and the other atomic spies had participated in one of the greatest conspiracies hatched during World War II – and one that has had the most long-lasting consequences.

INDEX

PICTURE CREDITS

Alamy: 32, 42, 50, 96, 152, 201, 212, 224, 246

Shutterstock: 67, 237

Wikimedia Commons: 10, 17, 23, 26, 27, 36, 48, 54, 59, 61, 71, 73, 77, 80 (x2), 83, 87, 93, 100, 109, 113, 119, 125, 126, 129, 131, 143, 147, 158, 165, 175, 183, 188, 197, 206, 210, 217, 222, 250